"This is a beautiful memoir. The photos alone offer a fascinating glimpse into the past, but Sharp's deft storytelling brings the people and animals into full color. She shows us a blended culture as well as the strong individuals that were so important to living on the edge and striving to make it work. My only criticism is that she sometimes holds back, giving us the bare bones of what must have been a complicated and sometimes painful story...so perhaps this isn't a criticism at all, but a recognition that the bones are all we need."

—Amy Hale Auker,
Author of *Rightful Place*,
Winner of 2012 WILLA, Creative Nonfiction

"You have created a beautiful and coherent story that teaches me about one ranch, but also about the life that existed in that area, the people—I feel as if I've had a fruitful experience that I didn't expect. And you have done honor to Lola and Pancho and your mother and all the human members of your extended family, as well as to Athena and Ty and the cattle and sheep. And the land. You have honored the land with your memories."

—Linda Hasselstrom,
Coauthor of *Dirt Songs: A Plains Duet*,
Winner of 2012 Nebraska Book Award, Poetry

A Slow Trot Home

John!

Keep Reading through Life!

Ruben, back in the day

A Slow Trot Home

LISA G. SHARP

Cover photo by Bob Sharp

All photos, except those noted, are used with the permission of © Bob Sharp.

Arizona and Santa Cruz County maps are courtesy of Michael Sharp.

San Rafael Cattle Company map is used by permission. Copyright © 2013 Esri. All rights reserved.

Author photo is courtesy of Matilda Essig.

A Slow Trot Home

Published by Wheatmark®
1760 East River Road, Suite 145, Tucson, Arizona 85718 U.S.A.
www.wheatmark.com

ISBN: 978-1-62787-074-0 (paperback)
ISBN: 978-1-62787-075-7 (ebook)
LCCN: 2013952404

rev201401

rev201402

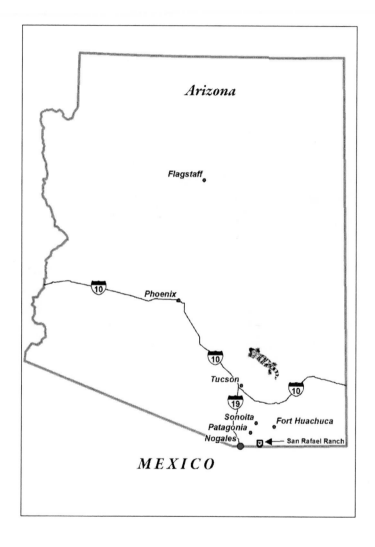

San Rafael Cattle Company headquarters

This book is dedicated to my two best friends,

my sons,

Michael and Charlie

Contents

Acknowledgments

Thank you to Heidi, Bill, Jean, Balinda, and Sally for all those writing, reading, and suggestion days.

Thank you to Linda Hasselstrom and Teri Markow — you gave me the courage to continue writing.

Thank you to Julia Moore for reading this so many times and your encouragement and friendship.

Thank you to my family for helping me with recollections and a special thanks to my brother, Bob Sharp, for photos from the old days.

Thank you to all the cowboys and ranchers I have known in my life. Their conversations, knowledge, and friendships will always be a part of me and are a part of this story.

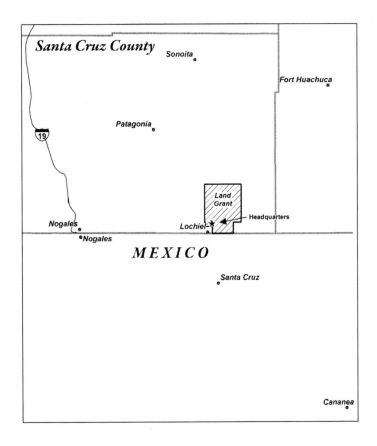

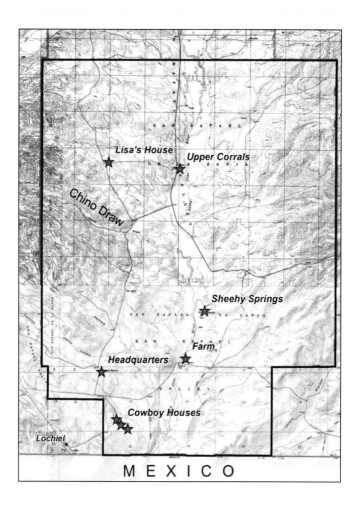

Lisa's House

Upper Corrals

Chino Draw

Sheehy Springs

Farm

Headquarters

Cowboy Houses

Lochiel

MEXICO

Arturo de la Ossa and José Mejía

Touchstone

Sometimes when driving in northern New Mexico, I see cattle grazing among pine trees or in small acequia-irrigated pastures next to adobe houses. Images of Black Baldies and Herefords come to mind but against a backdrop of grass-covered rolling hills spotted with Arizona live oak, manzanita bushes, and cottonwood trees. Once while camping in Valle Vidal north of Cimarron, New Mexico, I rode my horse through a green meadow dotted with blue and white penstemon and red paintbrush, and we crossed a rocky creek bed filled with rushing water from the previous night's summer rain. The memory of warm air coming off high desert grasses and wet dirt after a summer monsoon swept the New Mexico scents aside. Ranch memories flow like gravity's pull on water and soak my own body's soil.

The San Rafael Valley, 223 square miles of rolling short-grass rangeland in southeastern Arizona, is the template on which most of my life's experiences have been overlaid; it is a setting where my mind automatically goes when a sense is touched or a gut memory is tapped. This Valley is in eastern

Santa Cruz County, surrounded by the Nogales and Pata-gonia Mountains on the west and the Canelo Hills on the north. On the east side, the Huachuca Mountains' rugged peaks and juniper- and pine-covered canyons rise to 9,300 feet. To the south, the Valley continues into Mexico with the Santa Cruz River making its way and Mexican farms and apple orchards dotting the bottomland along the river's course.

Estate and family issues prompted my siblings and me to sell our family ranch, the San Rafael de la Zanja Land Grant, that our maternal grandfather bought in 1903. It had been part of the Greene Cattle Company that stretched deep into Sonora, Mexico, with its headquar-ters in Cananea, Sonora. After her mother's death, my mother traded her shares in the Greene Cattle Compa-ny's RO Ranch in Seligman, Arizona, for the San Rafael Cattle Company in Patagonia, and we started our move from California to Arizona in 1958. Eight years old then, I began spending summers at the ranch and school years in California. In 1963 I started high school in Arizona, and the ranch became my home.

Marriages and work took me away in 1973, but I never really left the ranch, most likely one of the reasons the marriages never worked out. My sons and I returned from California and New Mexico for every holiday and vacation until I moved back in 1993 to help care for Mom. After her death, I continued living there until August 17, 1999.

We signed the real estate sales agreement on December 22, 1998, and the ranch became another holding of The

Nature Conservancy (TNC), which in turn sold the head-quarters along with 3,700 adjacent acres to Arizona State Parks. The remaining 17,500 acres, TNC sold to a private landowner. I continued to live on the ranch's upper end until moving to Tubac, Arizona, eight months later.

That last night on the ranch, August 16, 1999, is impressed in me like a footprint on freshly poured concrete. The hours stretched to midnight, to one-thirty, then two-thirty. I sat in the window alcove surrounded by taped-up boxes in a barren house. My old dog, Athena, had died the week before, and the only animals remaining were three horses in the corrals who were soon to move with me to Tubac. It was probably the first time in our ranch's ninety-six-year history when no cows grazed nearby, and no occasional bawls could be heard.

The world around me was quiet and empty. Decades old scenes meandered through my mind as I gazed out into darkness and wanted only to touch memories: movies, cowboys, horses, farming, Mom, living a life on the Mexican border.

I thought about the Mexican cowboys from across "the line" who taught me how to ride and work cattle. Some came up with their families from the Cananea Ranch and lived in the cowboy houses. Others, who worked for us regularly, we picked up at *la línea* (the U.S./Mexico boundary line), which was, and still is in parts, a six-strand barbed wire fence. These cowboys stayed at the headquarters or bunked in one of the three cowboy houses south of the headquarters. They worked for a few months and then went back to their families in Mexico.

I opened all the house windows that night, feeling the muggy August air, knowing it wouldn't be duplicated anyplace else. I washed myself in all the ranch's senses, wanting to keep them with me: cold, hot, muggy, or dry, it didn't make any difference. Just infiltrate every cell, please.

The darkness hung on as I remembered the sheep grazing around the headquarters. A constant bb-a-a-a was in the air when Mom lived there. She bought 800 head from San Angelo, Texas, in the early 1960s, which caused more than a little stir in the Valley. Some neighbors stopped talking to us for a while. A few years later the movie *Heaven with a Gun*, starring Glenn Ford, was filmed at the ranch. It was a story about feuding cattle ranchers and sheepherders in the late 1800s and the preacher who brought peace. During the filming, we joked about the timing and said, "We should have had that preacher with us a few years ago and still need him now!"

Three o'clock. Four. The night's hours clicked by. The land's silence cradled me and the city-free world. As the horizon started to light up, all the familiar images appeared—low rolling hills covered with fading summer grama grasses, live oak trees, scrub black-bushes, and mountains. During my mother's last few weeks of life, she said, "I try to remember, Lees, the outline of the hills at the ranch. I can see them but can't get the lines to connect anymore." Will that happen to me as more years pass?

The previous day I walked up a small valley in Pasture 17 north of the house. Most Sunday mornings around 7:15, one or two fighter jets from Davis-Monthan Air Force Base in Tucson flew close to the house and continued up that valley. I'd wave from the yard, and they'd tip a wing and continue on their training course. Some Sundays, it was the only communication with civilization I'd have unless a lost driver traveled the one and one-half miles of rutted road up to the house. The last thing I'd tell the driver was, "Go back down the road, turn left at the corrals, and when you come to the "T," turn left again, and in ten or so miles you'll come to Patagonia."

Following a cow trail in the canyon, I dodged dried out old cow pies stuck to the dirt and noticed even the flies weren't interested in them anymore. Birds screeched ee-ee-ee, plukkkk, plukkkk as if scolding me for disturbing their morning siesta. Those sounds combined with the tops of sideoats and grama grasses sshhh'ing against my Levi's broke the all consuming silence. Sweat trickled down my back as one foot automatically swung in front of the other without a conscious destination.

The land's desolation slapped me. It didn't feel right anymore; it didn't feel whole or complete without a cow's bawl or a "git-up" yell of a cowboy moving cattle on the land. As acceptance sunk in that my time on the ranch had run out, I returned to the house—finally facing the plain and simple fact I'd known for months.

The sun wasn't shy as it came up over the Huachuca Mountains the next summer morning, and the temperature began a quick rise. Old Mr. Moore, a cattle buyer who came out to the ranch occasionally when I was young, used to say, "August is a miserable damn month—the dog days of summer, Lisa." August 17, 1999, fit that description: hot and miserable.

Friends, a few neighbors, and Ruben, a cowboy who stayed on the ranch, helped pack the U-Haul, I loaded my horses, and we left at 11:00 a.m. I drove the moving truck down the hill on the ranch's north end, turned left on the county dirt road, and let it carry me out of the Valley to a new house and a very different lifestyle. I thought about Mom, who managed the border ranch from 1958 until illness brought her down in 1988. That piece of land became my touchstone because of her; gratitude and sorrow billowed up side by side with dust from the road.

Each visit back to the San Rafael Valley area accentuates changes that have happened over the years. Another ranch has been sold, and I hear unfamiliar names living on familiar tracts of land. Most of my mom's generation has passed on, and I rarely recognize a face in the post office. Border security is foremost in everyone's mind, as opposed to the price of cattle. The perennial prayer, "I hope we have good summer rains," is said for water catchment barrels and landscaping, and for a majority of people, I imagine, cattle forage is not even a thought.

On our ranch, new fences have been put up, new wells drilled, and new families live there. These words were most likely said by the old-timers when we moved to the San Rafael Cattle Company. These changes I see make me write. I write to remember about growing up on a U.S./Mexico border ranch before fear replaced a welcome smile and a conversation with Mexican cowboys about their families and life in Mexico.

I write before we can no longer remember "the dark skies of Southern Arizona," a phrase referring to light pollution, which became common in the mid-1990s. I write before the wireless world and my age cause me to forget about waving to the mail lady as she drove on to the next ranch every Monday, Wednesday, and Friday, an era when box numbers and road signs weren't needed to get a letter.

I write to remember when cattle buyers and ranch owners weighed the cattle together, and a handshake sealed the deal. I write to remind myself about the time when we heard about a fall cattle sale that was done by video camera, and cowmen said, "Now, isn't that the damnedest thing you ever heard of?"

I write this for my mother, Florence Greene Sharp, to say thank you for giving me and my children memories of ranch life on the U.S./Mexico border.

Looking Through the Window

Sitting on the brown upholstered bench seat and fiddling with a steel pullout ashtray under the train's window, I watched desert images appear and disappear, one after another, like fanning pages in a picture book, not remembering the first or second or third image, yet being left with a complete picture in the mind. Desert scrub brush, Joshua tree cacti, sand, rocks, and telephone poles blended into the evening until the train's lights lit up the tracks. Eventually, the rhythmic rocking motion guided me to the upper berth in the Pullman car's compartment as Mom continued to read an Ellery Queen mystery magazine below.

From California to Mexico I traveled with my mother, interspersed with attending first through fourth grades in Southern California and receiving lessons from a tutor in Mexico. Then, Spanish flowed out of my mouth as easily as English. Throughout the 1950s and early 1960s, we boarded trains at the Los Angeles Union Station or the Alhambra Station and watched occasional lights from a lone structure break up desert darkness as the Southern Pacific Railroad cars carried us through Southern California and Arizona deserts. I never did understand why we would take the train to Arizona and fly back to Los Angeles, but we always did.

Hazy memories interspersed with blank splotches on a youth's timeline make up those early childhood years. Mom and Dad on the path of divorce, sisters and brother in boarding schools, and I, the youngest of the family, traveled with Mom.

Enrique, my grandmother's driver, waited on the platform as the train rolled into the Tucson station at 10:00 a.m. In the back seat of the Chevrolet, I half-listened to the grownups talk and looked at clouds silhouetted against Arizona blue skies while Enrique drove us along the highway past Benson and Fort Huachuca. We dropped into a canyon and stopped at The Copper Queen Hotel in Bisbee, Arizona. Ceiling fans blew warm air over us as I sipped orange juice and Mom drank black coffee with our lunch before we continued on to Mexico.

The U.S. Customs agent said, "Hello, Mrs. Sharp," as we passed through the border crossing station at Naco, Arizona.

"¡Hola Señora!"

Mom handed the Mexican customs agent a carton of cigarettes at Christmas time, and sometimes the official gave me a sugar cane stalk. We continued for another thirty-two miles of dirt roads to my grandmother's house while I chewed on the fresh sweet reed and gazed out the car window and looked at cattle grazing and cowboys riding. And roads . . . miles and miles of roads as dust swirled out behind us, a never-ending succession of pebbles drummed against the undercarriage while I hummed a tune, drifted off to sleep, and rode white fluffy elephants or horses in the sky.

After we passed a house enclosed by a wall covered with broken shards of glass on top, we entered the copper mining town of Cananea. Houses painted turquoise, pale pink, dirty white, or light brown replaced the pastureland. A small movie house and candy store on the corner marked our turn off the main road. After two more blocks of dirt roads, we drove over a cattle guard and up the drive to my grandmother's house, *La Casa Grande* (the Big House).

Brief scenes flash through my mind now. A cowboy lifts me up on my white horse, and I lope on hills around Cananea with another young girl whose parents work for the mine. Or the two of us ride through Cananea to my grandmother's house, stop at the candy store for a treat, and then search for a big rock to stand on to mount our horses. I walk down the steps of the house in the early evening and speak with Manuel, the night watchman, who always has an extra cup of super sweet *café con leché* (coffee with milk) to share. Easter egg hunts take place with cousins on the huge front lawn as parents watch, and I find a butterfly by a dyed egg to put in the collection I keep in our rooms at the Cananea house.

Each visit, we spent a few weeks there. A tutor came to the house, kept me up to date with my California school lessons, and I played in the afternoons while Greene Cattle

Company business occupied Mom. When it was time to leave, Enrique drove us back to the Tucson Airport in the blue and white Chevy, and I would peel the backs of my thighs off vinyl seats leaving sweat marks after the long drive. At LAX, a Yellow Taxi picked us up, turned off the freeway at the green exit sign marked HOLLYWOOD or in later years, PASADENA, and left us at our home to start the next day far away from the wide open spaces.

We were in Cananea when my grandmother died in 1955. Incense smoke floated over the mourners in the cathedral while all the family members walked by her coffin in front of the altar. A pallbearer lifted me up so I could kiss her powdered face with my five-year-old lips, and then I quickly reached for Mom's hand. After grandmother's death, estate issues surfaced, and family arguments and incomprehensible words zinged through the air. Over the next three years, Mom and Dad divorced, and estate lawsuits ensued.

After Mom traded her shares in the RO Ranch for the San Rafael Ranch, and my family began the transition from California to Patagonia. Mom was fifty-two years old in 1958 when she began to manage the 22,000-acre cattle ranch. She'd been raised in the cattle business in Mexico and while married lived on her family's ranch in northern Arizona. This life was not foreign to her or my brother and sisters. However, our family lived in Southern California when I was born. I had lived in a world of twenty-four hour electricity, phones, constant running water, and paved roads, sprinkled with drives to my mother's family home in Mexico equipped with all the modern conveniences. I knew changes were taking place in our lives when Enrique wasn't there to pick us up at the Tucson train station, and Mom drove a newly purchased car from Tucson to the ranch southeast of Patagonia, Arizona, that summer of 1958.

The pavement ended at the curve on McKowen Avenue, south of the current Family Health Center in Patagonia and from that point on, the washboard dirt road was hell on vehicles. Mom drove another eight miles, wound through small canyons, followed a stream bed, crested the narrow canyon's hill, and entered the San Rafael Valley. She had been to the ranch before, but it was all new to my eyes.

I felt we had arrived in a different universe, and civilization's flow did not have the strength to summit the hill, break the invisible barrier, and seep its way into this little part of planet Earth. The north end of the high Sonoran Desert, 223 square miles of rangeland, spread before us. The moment we entered the Valley, all the beauty of wide open spaces, blue skies, prairie grass, and grazing cattle—which had passed by me while I looked out car and train windows on our trips to Mexico—was held together in this one place by mountains and hills. When we reached the ranch headquarters twenty minutes later, I felt the big house wrap its arms around me like a king-size comforter on a twin bed.

Colin Cameron from Pennsylvania had moved west with investors' money in the 1850s and became a cattle baron in the Valley. After his two previous houses burned down, he finished building this house in 1898. The house reflected those found in the Midwest and South with arching brickwork over the windows and a wide porch. My grandfather bought Cameron's property in 1903, and it became part of the Greene Cattle Company ranch holdings.

The house stood proudly showing off its two and one-half stories of red brick made with dirt and sand from the Valley's floor. Like a soft-brimmed felt hat caught in a light wind, the brown shingle roof with its flat crown swept down over the porch. Mom and I climbed eight wood planks, each one long enough to hold four people, and we ascended to the wraparound veranda. Under the porch, basement windows let in whatever natural light could make its way through the forgotten dirt and dust encrusted panes.

I turned west and looked toward the barn and corrals. Dust floated in the air along with voices, but in other directions only quiet rangeland met my gaze. I peeked through wavy glass windows into the living room. A dark green leather couch and two matching leather chairs with tooled saddle designs on the pillows and wagon wheels for arm rests looked lonesome in the huge room. It didn't seem possible its single fireplace could begin to warm even a part of that expanse on a winter day.

The twenty-eight room house had seen its fair share of families and cowboys who sat at the breakfast table and drank coffee. At the time we arrived, a ranch manager and his family lived in the house. I knew we were only here for the day and would have to go to Nogales to spend the night, but I didn't want to leave.

"Lees, why don't you go on down to the barn and see what's going on?"

"Why aren't we staying here?" I asked hopefully.

"The ranch manager lives here for now and we'll be driving out daily," Mom said.

"Oh. Well, when can we stay?"

"I don't know, we'll have to work it all out," a familiar phrase I was to hear all my life.

Heaven awaited me on the other side of the sturdy wood corral boards. Cowboys doctored a few cows with dust-induced pinkeye, each cow received a poof of pink powder in her eye, a "kaboom-b" banged each time the steel gate fell down, and the cows scrambled out of the chute in search of their calves. Two horses with reins looped loosely over the fence waited patiently, each with heads down, one hind leg slightly bent ignoring the commotion around them.

One of the barn's tall adobe walls had names carved haphazardly on it—marks left by cowboys who had come and gone. And then I walked into a room with smells I recognized from Cananea. I breathed aromas of leather and horse sweat. I looked at the indispensable tools of a cowboy that lined the tack room. Multicolored saddle blankets and brown pads covered saddles that sat on wood forms, which protruded from the wall. Stirrups dangled in the air avoiding the lucky mice that escaped the barn cats' claws. Bridles and reins hung from hooks in the low rafters, and my small fingers stroked the reins—the soft brown leather had spent more days on horses' necks than I'd been alive—that I knew.

As I touched the saddles and reins, looked at the spurs on the wall, heard the bellows of cows, and imagined horseback riding over the hills, I felt a peace I'd never known before. *Justin Morgan Had a Horse, My Friend Flicka, Smokey*, and all the other horse books that lined my bookshelves in my California bedroom came to life in that isolated childhood moment.

The traveling in my early years, propelled by wheels and engines, was about to be replaced by four legs that would carry me over grasslands, hills, and into arroyos. I became a part of that world as easily as that first shoot of spring grass that finally made its way above ground.

I was home.

More Dirt than Grass

I can only imagine what Mom must have gone through when we arrived at the San Rafael headquarters on that summer day in June 1958.

From the porch of the big house, she looked at the country spread around her. Far to the south, the Cananea Mountain top would say hello, and she thought about growing up in that mining town where her father started his mining and cattle operations in the late 1800s. Feelings of nostalgia perhaps and sadness most likely spread across her emotional map. Memories and her parents' gravestones in Mexico were the only connections left after a seventy-year family legacy of mining and ranching. All the words said at roundtable discussions and estate arguments, words that could never be taken back, heightened the melancholia, but at that minute, thoughts of the responsibilities before her replaced emotion. She sighed deeply, almost as if her body said, "Here we go again," and leaned against the brick walls.

She heard her youngest daughter humming a tune, and the little girl rocked back and forth in a dilapidated wood rocker on the porch's west end. The wide covered porch with its faded paint and warped wood floorboards begged for maintenance. She hoped it didn't cave in while Lees was sitting down there.

"Lees, why don't you go to the barn and see what's going on?"

Summer rains hadn't started yet, and the rangeland looked pretty damn desolate. More dirt than grass at this point, she thought. She, divorced and fifty-two years old, needed to learn every aspect of the ranch and raise her four children, ages eight to nineteen, alone.

Bum Hip

My horses are living the rest of their days at a friend's ranch in the Valley. I stopped riding in 2010, too much pain. The hips aren't "stove-up," as cowboys say; no, the edges of the hip bone are "just plain wore-out." Parts of my hands are permanently calloused—edges of the forefingers and thumbs where reins used to lie don't look much different from weathered thin bark on a dying tree. The rest of the hands aren't much better. They're covered with sun spots and lined, like someone took a fork and ran the tines back and forth in all directions and hoped to come up with a design. The two of them look like they've run life's course, and it's time for replacement models to be introduced.

I don't remember my first ride, no more than when I took my first steps. Now, though, when life nags me, I close my eyes and move my thumbs softly over the callouses. I feel a horse underneath me, that slow, steady walk on a dirt trail, blue sky above, pores opening and absorbing the sun. Today, that is my meditation.

A friend of mine, during the last hours of her mother's

life, walked to the corrals, rubbed her hands all over her horse, and then cupped them over the dying woman's nose. The old woman smiled, whispered, "Thank you," and placed her own hand over her daughter's as she closed her eyes for the last time.

You don't forget. That smell is as recognizable as bread baking in the oven. I don't think that scent ever left Mom either. She told me when she and my father were married, she loved to ride her mare on the RO Ranch in northern Arizona. Her tall, lean body relaxed with two activities: playing the piano and riding. We never played a duet and we rode together only once.

It was 1958. Pancho, a ranch cowboy, saddled the horse with Mom's English Event saddle. I watched the woman as she stepped on the wood block, put her foot in the metal stirrup, mounted the horse with a deep groan, and bent over the horse's neck for a minute. That busted hip from a childhood fall and injured back from an old horse accident, combined with terrible circulation problems in her legs, told her that her riding days were over. But not quite yet her mind said, and she sat up tall and headed for the corral gate. I was eight years old and ecstatic: I was riding the white horse, and I was riding with my mother for the first time *ever*.

Mom's light gray knit pants met the top of old jodhpur boots, and a loose white cotton blouse protected her skin from the Arizona sun. Bits of silver sparkled in her dark brown hair that grazed the top of the pale blue silk scarf, which covered her neck. Within minutes, an errant shock of prematurely white hair fell on one side of her sunglasses. The fifty-two-year-old woman sat on the animal as if she could ride all day while her eyes scanned the pastures and scrutinized the cattle. Pancho rode beside her with his hand tucked inside his chap's side pocket, his sixty-foot *reata* (rawhide plaited rope) lay on his horse's shoulder. Ranch owner and cowboy talked about cows, fences, and windmills as the cowboy's spurs sang a soft tune to his horse's hoofbeats. Not caring about cow numbers, overgrazed pastures, lack of rain or windmills, I loped my old pony over well-worn cow trails and tasted heaven.

We headed back as the horses in the pony trap wandered past us to the drinker for their evening water. Mom unsuccessfully stifled a groan as she dismounted. She never rode again but that didn't stop her from checking on ranch work. It never made a difference where the work was being done. Whether it was building new fences or drilling new wells, she checked on the progress. After a pasture had been rounded up, she sat in the truck and pointed out which cows to cull from the herd or which registered bull to put with the cows. The noise of a truck engine followed by a trail of dust on the county road or a pasture's two-track road caused the Mexican cowboys to say, *"Aquí viene la Patrona"* (Here comes the Boss Lady).

Now I walk in the New Mexico mountains, following paths with figures on bicycles, walkers with sticks, and equestrians that embellish Share the Trail signs and am glad to be hemmed in by piñons, juniper and ponderosa pines and away from cars and concrete. Seeing the world from the level of a horse's eye, I think how recklessly I rode— there weren't any obstacles, just ways to go over, up, and around them—learned that from watching the cowboys and hearing, "Well, let's figure it out."

I quickly detect sounds of hoofbeats and step aside. After the riders pass, I continue walking and breathing the familiar lingering smells before they dissipate in the mountain air.

Too Young

Ten days had passed since San Juan's Day and true to tradition, the rains started on June 24. Legend holds that on that day in 1540, the explorer Francisco Vasquez de Coronado stood by the Santa Cruz River, prayed for rain, and the clouds opened up. It was 11:00 a.m this summer of 1962, and the monsoon season hit the Valley like clockwork. Pancho and I sat in the barn as rain drops chattered incessantly on the tin roof; unrelenting torrents obliterated views of the big house, hills, and even the road in front of the barn.

Arturo, Enrique, and Oscar, the ranch's farmers, stacked a cutting of alfalfa in the barn the day before, and there were still a few hay bales left on the wood-planked hay trailer. Pancho pulled some down, and the two of us looked like sports fans sitting on bleachers waiting for a predictable game to be over.

Batwing chaps, their leather stained a deep chocolate with cows' blood, urine and shit, covered the cowboy's legs. Frayed edges dusted his boot tips; his heels rested on the concrete floor. My boot heels met the air. I was living the life I read about in children's horse books. It couldn't get much better.

Tall adobe walls with various shelves drilled into their soft bricks enclosed us on three sides. Gas cans, a few forty-gallon oil barrels, shovels, stiff rubber fire-flaps, and a wheelbarrow leaned against the mud brick walls. Thunder booms echoed off the tin roof and around wood ceiling beams as errant rain drops rode the odd gust of wind that sped through an open passageway, the water splattering on the concrete floor. The air felt good, cool and moist, and the pungent smell of fresh-cut alfalfa took my mind to the farm.

Arturo taught me to drive the tractor that summer. He lived in Lochiel, a little town just south of the ranch on the Mexican border, and had worked on the ranch for years. We sat on two oil-stained corduroy cushions, which covered a spring-exposed tractor seat. My hands became invisible under his as he showed me how to steer the green John Deere tractor. If the turn was too sharp, I'd hear the cowboys groan as they watched stacked bales fall off the hay wagon, "...y no quieres ese, Lisa" (and you don't want that), he told me.

Up and down the rows we went, and since my legs couldn't reach the clutch, the slow deliberate speed never changed. I'd look around and see a cowboy brush flecks of hay and dust off his face or lift his hat off as he ran the crook of his arm over his forehead to clear sweat, all the while walking to the next bale. After the men had placed a foundation of hay on the trailer, we'd be ready for the next five or six rows, each lined with seventy- to eighty-pound compacted green bricks. The cowboys' feet kept a steady cadence with the tractor's pace—step, step, step, lift and toss, step, step . . .

When the trailer was full, Arturo got on the tractor. I jumped off so he could drive it to the hay barn over cut fields and raised borders while the men's bodies took a rest on the back of the trailer. I heard them laugh as they said, *"Hoy somos milperos, mañana estaremos vaqueros"* (Today we're farmers, tomorrow we will be cowboys).

I looked for metates or manos in the fields as I walked back to my horse who had been grazing on the cut stems. Arturo found most of them though, brought them up to the house and the centuries-old Indian grinding stones lined the walkway at the ranch headquarters.

A bolt of lightning hit the pasture in front of the barn; I forgot about the farm and looked up at Pancho. I asked him in Spanish, "What are you doing?"

A Prince Albert tobacco tin, a little box of wood matches and a small stiff-sided envelope filled with flimsy white paper lay on his chaps. His hands, calloused and scarred, pulled out some papers from the envelope.

"Un cigarrito, Lisa."

I'd been riding with Pancho every summer for the past four years, trailing him on my old white horse, helping him, or in some instances hindering him, which probably happened more times than I'd ever know. We'd stop in the middle of a dry, sandy section on the Santa Cruz River. He'd get on one knee, scoop sand out of a spot, and soon, a pool of clear water would appear. His brown face crinkled as he smiled and said, *"Aqua,"* pointing to the puddle. I'd get off the horse and have a cool drink. All the while, he'd have a cigarette dangling out of his mouth as he mounted his horse and sat with his two hands on the saddle horn patiently waiting for me to get a drink.

When it got close to lunch time, he'd find a nice big oak tree with a gnarly old root knot at its base and lay out lunch. Our horses, grateful to be out of the sun, would stand quietly with their heads down, the reins looped lightly on a tree's overhead branch. After he'd unwrap a burlap-covered bundle tied on the back of his saddle, we'd have bean burritos with a few strips of chile inside homemade tortillas. But before he ate, he'd pinch his cigarette out and put it aside on the tree's root knot.

"Mas tarde, Lisa" (For later).

Had there been others around, they could have set their watches by our summer routine.

Pancho talked about the cows or calves as cigarette ashes fell into his cupped hand, the reins dangling over his forefinger. We spent lots of hours in silence, jogging slowly through pastures, looking at cattle as he wrote cow registration numbers in his black leather book. If a few head needed to be moved, a fence worked well as the third cowboy. I rode drag and looked at the cows' tails, and Pancho rode along their sides.

We crossed the border a few times through a small gate by the river. He knew the cowboy who worked the neighboring ranch on the Mexican side; he'd help us bring a stray cow back, or we'd move one of his cows back over. Sometimes we'd just sit and visit.

Cigarettes appeared out of Pancho's snap button shirt pocket; he'd strike a match on the side of his Levi's, palm the lit match, inhale, blow on the flame, and drop the blackened wood stick back in the shirt pocket—all in one easy motion. If the wind blew, his brown felt hat provided some protection and again, he cupped the flame as a wisp of smoke soon swept through his fingers.

I didn't know a person could make a cigarette. Mom smoked Viceroys, which came in cellophane-wrapped boxes.

"Get me a cigarette, Lees," she'd say as she drove.

I'd pull a red tab, the plastic slipped away and perfectly shaped filtered cigarettes appeared, lined up three deep under their foil covering like soldiers in formation.

I watched this Mexican cowboy as he made a cigarette in about ninety seconds. He ran the papers over his tongue; two flimsy sheets of paper became one. As he tapped the can with his forefinger, tobacco spilled out into the small white paper trough he held between his fingers. With his thumbs guiding the paper up and over the tobacco as the index and middle finger provided the wall, a little tube appeared and again, he ran his tongue over the paper's edge and pressed it in place with a finger. Not one speck of tobacco dropped. With not a crinkle in the paper, an even diameter from end to end, the cigarette lay on his palm.

I wanted to try and asked as much, but he put the tobacco can in his chaps along with the papers and said, *"Erés demasiado joven"* (You're too young).

The rain finally stopped. Pancho covered his balding

head with his sweat-stained, droopy brown cowboy hat that made me think it was time to let the wind blow it away. My white horse followed the bay gelding as we left the corrals and rode into the sloppy pasture. Water ran in rivulets around bunch grass that blocked any steady flow and eventually formed puddles in different cavities on the ground. Our horses' hoofs sucked up mud with each step; we heard *plop* as each hoof hit the ground and the sound of the earth inhaling as the hooves left the mud. I knew where we were going. We'd been doing this same thing a couple of times a week for the last month.

We found the old bull at the west end amid century plants and agave cactus stalks. His sons and daughters grazed close to their moms on surrounding hills. The once-1800 pound Hereford bull had had a cancer scraped off his eye a month before, and it still wasn't doing well. His horns, trained with small weights at an early age, were symmetrical in size and angle in their curve around his forehead and were about the only thing left on him that looked elegant, if such a term could be applied to a big ol' bull. Scruffy-looking brown hide now hung over his bones like an afterthought.

He remained on the ground as we dismounted, turning his head a little further to get a better look with his good eye. The milky orb soon dribbled with an anti-septic solution, becoming yellow as we squirted medicinal powder on the lids and eyeball. The fly repellant Pancho sprayed stopped the pesky insects from irritating the animal even more. Poncho untied the burlap bag on his saddle and emptied grain on the ground.

We didn't have to rope him. He was a gentle old man. That day, we both saw that maggots had found a home.

"*Ay, es malo*" (Oh, it's bad).

Later that week though, I was allowed to see the old bull shot, watch his big head fall on the ground, and hear the last breath leave his body as his jaw opened. The maggots weren't in the line of fire, and they continued to burrow. One squirmed out of the infected eye socket and traveled on down to his nose, but Pancho flicked it off and stepped on it, hard.

"Bury the bull, Pancho," Mom said.

The cowboys shook their heads in disbelief when they heard their orders.

"I can't leave him for the buzzards, Lees. Not this one," she said to me.

We stood on the porch and watched as the John Deere tractor moved the bull and covered him with dirt. The next summer a few sprigs of range grass and weeds covered the mound. I rode by his resting place and thought of all those registration papers we filled out listing Mill Iron as the sire. It was my first experience of watching a death occur, one of my many small steps out of childhood as I held Mom's hand that day on the porch of the big house.

Pancho, Michael, and John Hays

No Fear

In the early 1960s, the white horse died. Age finally got him. In Cananea, he would wait quietly for me to finish brushing him, whether he needed it or not. At San Rafael Ranch, I would step on a water trough's metal side and throw myself on the old horse's back, digging my right heel into his ribs that gave me the needed leverage to get astride. The cowboys would stand by the tack room door and slowly shake their heads as they walked over to us. One might mutter, *"que paciencia"* (what patience) and stroke the old gelding's neck.

Sometimes the horse would turn his head, his long gray forelock angling down over his face, and look at me as if to say, "Now, what are you doin'?" and redistribute his weight to balance the circus act out. He defined a kid's horse and was my best friend during those first summers in Arizona.

Mom told me the night before that a new bunch of horses were coming up from Mexico and no doubt from the commotion we heard at daybreak, they had arrived at the barn. I ran out of the house and down to the barn. A small stout red chestnut horse with white stockings and a thick white blaze, which ran from forelock to muzzle, stood by the tack room.

"*¿Qué te parece, Lisa?*" (What do you think?) Pancho asked.

This was the kind of horse I saw in merry-go-rounds!

"Candy. Peppermint candy."

"*¿Dulce?*" Pancho said.

"Candy," I repeated.

"Kound-ay," he said and finally the name *"El caballito de Lisa"* (Lisa's little horse) stuck with the gelding.

Chito, another cowboy from the Cananea Ranch, brought a saddle from Cananea for me. It had tooled flowers on the sienna leather cantle and stirrup fenders and silver conchos that held long latigo strings, which hung down just far enough to keep flies off either side of the horse's belly. Horse and saddle gleamed under the sun.

I had graduated.

The kid's saddle hung from the tack room's ceiling, and a "real" saddle took its place on one of the saddle racks. Problem was the saddle was so heavy, I couldn't lift it onto the horse—lots of years of bareback riding followed unless someone was around to help me hoist up that piece of leather.

The two of us trotted from one end of the Valley to the other. I picked blackberries, apples, and pears in the old orchard east of the farm during the summer while the little gelding grazed. Occasionally, I took fruit over to the Ashburns, a neighboring ranch family. Helen made the best blackberry and apple pie. It wasn't much of a coincidence when I showed up at their place a day or two later, tied my horse by the low brick wall, and walked down the brick path to the front door.

"Hello, Lisa. Did you get those apples from the orchard?"

"Yes."

"They say Mrs. Cameron brought apple and pear seedlings from Pennsylvania when they came out in the late 1800s. She got the cowhands to plant the trees there by Sheehy Springs in that orchard. Did you see all those wood racks in the basement of the big house? Well, those were for drying apples and pears."

On the weekends, I said, "Hello" to people from both sides of the border who were having an afternoon picnic under the big apple trees. Families from Santa Cruz, Mexico, drove up for a Sunday picnic and picked the fruit for *empanadas* (small dough-covered pies), and neighbors stopped by the orchard to pick berries for their jam and jelly canning—everyone knew about the orchard tucked down into the small draw.

My favorite place to ride was up to Duquesne, an old ghost town west of the ranch, six or so miles up the road. We met early day hippies, wanna-be prospectors, and I-heard-about-this-place tourists from town. Candy stepped over tin Log Cabin syrup cans, mangled forks and spoons, cracked plates with little blue and pink flowers—remnants of a boom town gone bust in the 1920s. The horse shied away from open wells but sniffed wild irises, which still grew in forgotten gardens.

After one of these rides, I walked up to the big house and saw Mom standing on the porch.

"Where did you go this time?"

"Duquesne. I went up a small valley on my way up there and found an old graveyard. The tombstones had dates from the early 1900s, and most were for kids, Mom."

"They must have died of an epidemic. You have to tell me where you are going, Lees. Nobody ever knows when you take off or where you go. You've been gone for hours."

I never thought about that. I was just a kid without fear.

Lights Go On

Looking at an old photo of the big house, I find it isn't hard to envision Mom's early years there.

Mom lit the kerosene lamp by her bed quietly as Lisa slept in the bedroom's other twin bed. She wanted to read; it helped her relax in the morning before she started the day. As a faint outline of the barn and machine shop made its way through the darkness, the bathroom light began to glow, which signaled one of the cowboys who lived in the basement had turned on the Koehler generator. The woman started coffee in the little kitchen and rotated an orange half on the glass juicer.

Most mornings, her legs weren't swollen from the lymphedema. She had learned to live with it as it progressed over the years; support hose eased the pain from enlarged calves and ankles, and orthopedic shoes gave the needed support. After a morning of walking to the barn, driving to the farm, or checking on cows, she would lie down on the bed for a half-hour with her swollen feet and legs elevated on a bolster cushion. This morning, her legs didn't ache and she hadn't been up long enough for the swelling to start, so she leaned against the little kitchen's counter and waited for the coffee to finish perking on the small white enamel stove.

When she first moved into the house, she wondered why there were two kitchens and decided there must have been one for the cowboys and one for the ranch manager. She was grateful for the small one next to her bedroom regardless of the reason. It was so much easier to use this kitchen in the early morning, and it was warmer than the big kitchen.

Black binders embossed with American Hereford Association lay stacked on the kitchen's square oak table. Near them were four registration papers, all clipped together, with a note "POSSIBLE SHOW PEN FOR PHOENIX LIVESTOCK SHOW?" Lined ledger sheets on the table's corner waited for the May 1963 listing of expenses. She looked at the accounting sheets and thought there was no income to list—no cows went to auction this month—just expenses. She ignored the constant pull of paperwork and walked through the sparsely furnished living room into the big kitchen on the house's northeast side.

A puff of stale warm air hit her face as she pushed open the swinging door. Immediately these thoughts rose in her mind: new windows needed to be put in here; every door in the house needed oil and weather-stripping. If I got some shades for the east windows and stopped that unrelenting sun, it would be cooler in the summer. The enclosure of the sun porch was the next house project, and she made a mental note. If I made that sun porch a dining room, put the dining room table there, decent windows, I could do paperwork, talk to the cowboys and visitors, plus get a view of the valley. This house would be a never-ending project, she concluded and walked back into the living room.

She looked at the mixture of the ranch's oak furniture and the recently bought Sears furniture in the living room, and the words "house maintenance" pulsed in her mind with more items to add to the lengthening list: rooms needed paint, bedrooms needed carpets, fix up the . . . where to start? She returned to her bedroom to get ready for the day.

At 7:30 a.m. she began the paperwork, heard the door swing open between the big kitchen and living room and the echo of boots on the wood floor.

"*¿Señora?*"

"*Aquí estoy, Ramon, en la cocina chica*" (Here I am . . . in the little kitchen).

The cowboy took off his hat, sat down, and the conversation immediately went to lack of rain, where to move the cattle in the eaten-down pastures, what day to get the registered calves' weaning weights . . . another day.

Looking southeast from the ranch to Mexico

RO mare with her colt

Spring

Windmills spun like out-of-control Ferris wheels and pumped water into cattle troughs. The overflow gushed out of pipes into dug-out dirt water tanks, and the water rippled with tiny waves.

The sun woke up earlier and went to bed later while roots inhaled morning dew. The Valley's grasses relished the warmth, and their foliage turned pale green. Yellow, blue, and white wildflowers whose names I didn't know looked like polka dots on the gunnysack tinged landscape.

Blue herons began to stake their land by the river, and water tanks and ducks took off for cooler climes. Cows hunkered down in the pasture and faced east to avoid the western wind. Animal butts received the wind, and cowboys rode with their heads tilted towards the blasts of air as they made their circle. The dry air sucked the moisture and by late spring, brittle grass remained.

Newborn calves explored a world around their mama's hoofs and suckled swollen teats. Peach-fuzz hides covered spindly legs, and tummies felt familiar muzzles and tongues.

"Good calf crop?"

"Whew, wet spring."

"Never seen so many wildflowers."

"Windy spring brings summer rains, right?"

"Sure as hell better if we have to put up with this."

"Heifer died calving, coyotes took 'em both."

Cattle heard the ranch truck's horn *honk-honk* and started to trot out of canyons and run down hills across the flatland, eager to eat the leafy alfalfa flakes of hay. A cowboy balanced on the truck's bed, as it bounced over the pasture, flipping one flake after another over the truck's side.

The horse tossed his head wanting to join the cattle and eat the protein rich cottonseed cake pellets, which dribbled on the scattered hay. Baby calves couldn't keep up with their mamas running, so they stood alone and bawled. Mamas left 'em for fresh feed. Give 'em time and they would all be together again, cows eating and calves suckling, I thought, as I softly urged my horse on.

Salt

Each breath we took brought in tiny particles of earth and dust as Mom backed the truck into the farm's hay barn. PLUNK. I tossed another alfalfa bale on the truck's bed. Thank you gravity, for doing ninety-nine percent of the work. Stack the bales so they don't fall off into the pasture. Mantras for loading hay in the truck automatically ran through my mind. Be careful, though, never know what you'll find. Once we found two bobcat kittens hidden in the hay. That woke us up on that morning! Mama must have left them to get water and food. Cute little things, from a distance.

I knocked on the cab's roof to signal—ready to go. We started to head out on an early winter morning to feed the registered herd in Pasture 6. After going a couple of feet, the truck stopped.

"I left my dark glasses on one of the bales, Lees," I heard as she opened the door to get them.

A minute or so passed.

"Lees!"

From the truck's bed, I saw my sixty-three-year-old mother flat on the ground. Running over to her, I looked at the ripped gray pant leg and saw blood dribbling down her calf.

"What happened?"

"I bumped against something. Help me get up."

She moved her five-foot-nine-inch frame onto her hands and knees, reached for my hand, and hoisted herself up as I braced myself against the hay bales. Looking down, I saw a threaded metal bolt with fabric still attached sticking out of one of the tall black steel supports, which held up the barn's roof.

"We gotta get you into town and see Dr. Mock."

"Just get me to the house. I want to look at it and clean it out before I do anything. God only knows what kind of infection could set in on these poor ol' broken-down legs."

We maneuvered up the steps with her arm over my shoulder, onto the porch and into the house, through the living room and finally, reaching the little kitchen, she sat. Her left leg, extended on a chair, looked like a sausage ready to split its casing. I caught my breath when I saw the ragged hole, three-quarters of an inch in diameter surrounded by red discoloration and oozing blood.

"Get some water and some salt."

"Mom, we have got to go to town."

"Get the damn water, Lisa."

"OK."

"Hold that bowl under my leg while I pour this on the hole."

She pushed on her leg to force more blood out of the wound as the trickling water became red and fell into the bowl.

"Get me more water, please."

Same procedure again.

"Now, the salt."

I did as told.

She put some salt into the warm water and spilled it all over her leg.

"Aaagh," came out of my mouth.

"Lisa, how else am I going to clean this out right now?" she said impatiently. "Just hold the bowl to catch the water."

I found a bottle of Mercurochrome and poured some on a piece of gauze so the wound would be covered. Before I was able to put it on her leg, though, Mom pulled the bottle from my hand and poured the red antiseptic directly into the hole. She straightened up on the chair and let out a muffled, "Damn."

"Now, put the gauze on it, wrap my leg, and let's get into town."

Doc Mock swiveled around on his round green vinyl-covered stool and said, "Well, Mrs. Sharp, this is going to take a while to heal. Stay off it."

His first sentence was correct. His instructions, "Stay off of it," didn't happen. I imagine he knew that the instructions were going to the wind since he was a country doctor who had driven all over eastern Santa Cruz County, delivering babies at ranch homes and stitching up every kind of cut in the world, knowing ranchers said "OK" but kept doing what they had been doing the day before. It took four months for the wound to heal from the inside out, and doctors always asked, "What happened to that leg there?"

"Just a cut," she'd say and continue with the conversation.

House's Center

My gut was tense and gurgling, my neck stiff as re-bar. Instinctively, I knew this was the last one, the last time, the last Christmas at the ranch. How many had I spent here? Every Christmas, except maybe three, and this was 1997.

Real estate papers hadn't been signed yet; nothing had been decided. I saw people in town or neighbors on the road and the elephant—Have you sold the ranch?—was always in the air, though the words were never spoken. I said to myself do not think about it. Instead, savor this moment, hear my family laugh, enjoy the Christmas atmosphere.

Sitting by the wood stove in the big kitchen, I asked my body to relax. The room was warm and breakfast smells lingered in the air. Family conversations in the living room faded as I traveled in the nooks and crannies of life held in this room.

A red-checkered oil cloth covered the wood table. A small blue glass pitcher on the table top held pine sprigs and pyracantha sprigs still laden with red berries. Daffodils filled the tiny vase in spring, marigolds followed in summer, and dried grass in the autumn months—the little glass calendar had been around since we moved into the house in 1960.

That summer, Mom and I walked across the line to do some shopping and bought some glasses and dinner plates, and she picked up this little pitcher from the store's shelf. It had a glass stopper; she thought it would be good for pouring salad dressing. The stopper broke at some point, and the pitcher remained in the table's center, empty for a few days. Then, someone put a couple of marigolds in it and another small habit began, consciously at first, then simply became part of the kitchen routine.

The redwood wainscot paneling surrounding the kitchen walls looked good after being stripped in the 1960s of various colors of oil paints that had been applied over the house's ninety-odd-year history. It should look good, should look DAMN good, as a matter of fact. My sisters and brother, carpenters and cowboys, guests and movie crews—every minute we weren't doing something, Mom put us to work stripping the paint off the wood and the doors and cleaning every brass door plate and knob on the redwood doors in the house's middle floor. By the time it was all done, if none of us ever heard the words "California redwood" again, it would have been just fine.

"Do you know I found a glass of water almost frozen in the big kitchen this morning?" my sister said in 1965. A Franklin wood stove was installed next to the gas cook stove.

In the mid-1960s, a big diesel generator replaced a DC-only Kohler generator, giving us AC power twenty-four hours a day. A hand held electric beater sat on the counter. Long gone were the days of making chocolate chip cookies by hand: letting the butter soften, sprinkling in the sugar a little at a time, then adding the eggs—we did all the steps slowly so the dough would be easy to beat.

There had been plants and a few chairs on the screened-in sun porch on the kitchen's east side when we moved into the house. The old sun room had been enclosed and was ready to accommodate our family dining table and chairs. In 1966, our house sold in California, and I remembered when the two moving company trucks loaded with our furniture showed up at the ranch that summer. That particular day distinctly stayed with me because it was my first recollection of racial prejudice against the Mexican people.

It was a hot June day. Not a breeze, not a cloud. Cottonwood leaves hung motionless from their stems and short nubs of grass crackled under boots. The heat forced the body to work in slow motion. A semi truck with California license plates pulled up alongside the house and left a shroud of dust in the air too worn out to continue falling to the ground. Two khaki clad men climbed out of the cab and looked around.

"Who in the hell lives out here?" I heard as I walked down the porch steps.

"I do. My family does. Ranchers do."

"Well, we have furniture, but it sure ain't gonna fill that house. God, it's hot here."

Well, it's gonna get hotter, I thought, so you better have something to wipe that sweat off your faces.

A couple of the cowboys came up from the barn, and we started to unload the semi. We walked up the front porch steps with boxes, mattresses, and household items in the ninety degree mid-morning heat. Mom stood in the living room's archway and directed us where to put what. We didn't speak much, just trudged along, unloaded the truck, and hoped we were done by lunchtime.

The dining area finally looked complete. Our oval oak table and six chairs with cane seats stood in the center on a red and white rug from Jacome's, a store in Tucson. An old Dutch sink and one side table finished the room.

With a sandwich and a big jug of iced tea for everyone, I walked over to where the cowboys sat in the truck's shade and joined them for lunch. The drivers were inside the half-empty trailer leaning against one side. I thought they must be sweltering in there, wondered why they weren't outside, but kept my mouth shut and sat down next to José. The cowboys and I talked about the furniture and weather. Jokes were made about who would stay to help unpack everything as all eyes moved and looked at me. I overheard the truck drivers' conversation and was grateful the cowboys didn't understand English.

"How come she's sitting with them. They're Mexicans."

"She was probably raised with them."

"Well, my kid wouldn't be out there. She'd be with her own kind."

"Listen to her; she talks just like them."

"Let's finish up and get outta here."

I hope you don't come back either, I thought, as we got up to finish the job.

Ranch oak dressers blended with my maternal grand-mother's furniture. Fabric upholstered couches and chairs replaced leather couches and chairs with the wagon-wheel arm rests. The Chinese scroll that was in the Pasadena house living room now hung in the hall. The big house had transitioned to our home in an afternoon.

I heard someone talking in the office and for a while, I listened to the conversation, but soon I was lost in thought as I remembered my sister's wedding on a November day in 1969.

Mastering the Art of French Cooking, Gourmet Vol. l and *The Joy of Cooking* lay on the kitchen table. For two weeks, Janie, my sister, Beatrice, Mom's housekeeper, and I had supported the U.S. dairy industry. We used dozens of eggs and gallons of cream in an effort to bake the perfect white cake for Mary's wedding. Finally, two layers, each one with a nice pie-shaped wedge cut out of it, sat in the middle of the table. The three of us agreed the layer on the right was the winner. Frosting was next.

Rum frosting, plain buttercream frosting, orange rum flavored frosting. We tried them all and again, used pounds of butter. Rum frosting won the taste test. Beatrice had just completed a cake decorating correspondence course, and she piped samples of pink roses with green stems and leaves through a fluted tube on patches of wax paper. We decided on the decorations. The cake was assembled and ready on the wedding day.

Mary and John, the groom, stood in the dining room framed by oatmeal tinted rangeland that stretched out under a canopy of blue sky outside the big windows. With hands entwined, the newly married couple held Mom's monogrammed silver cake knife ready to cut the three layer wedding cake, which set in the middle of the family oak dining table. The traditional cake was beautiful with piped white roses on all layers, frosting ribbons on the sides with a small plastic bride and groom on top. Beatrice had made a special trip into town with one of the cowboys to find that decoration for *her* cake.

As guests watched, the couple started to cut the pastry. But in seconds we heard a soft *tap*. The silver knife only went down one inch. John looked at Mary, Mary looked at Janie and me; we walked to the table as Mary scraped some of the buttercream frosting away to reveal a hard white plastic circle.

Beatrice, a five-foot-one-inch Mexican woman, with tiny hands that made the best green corn tamales ever, was dressed in pink and stood by the kitchen cupboards. She walked over and joined us at the table. She told us with a beaming smile that she didn't want to have any of the cake crumbs get in the frosting or spoil the piped cake decorations, so she had placed a plastic disk not only on the bottom of each tier to hold the cake, but on top of each tier as well. It allowed easier spreadability of the icing.

The three of us looked at Beatrice, back at one another, and for ten seconds, thoughts of "Are you kidding ME?"

scrambled quickly through our brains. We chuckled a little. What else can you do? She had worked so hard to display the perfect cake.

We dismantled the pastry and served it without the top layer of frosting. Beside the layers were the round plastic tops with a panorama of beautiful piped flowers, stems, and leaves. We saved the smallest cake, wrapped and frozen, to be cut by John and Mary on their first anniversary and covered its icing layer separately with the Saran wrap securely pressed to the plastic disk.

I stood up, threw a piece of oak in the wood stove, and walked over to the kitchen window. I saw the very top of Mt. Wrightson to the north. The old timers told us that on summer mornings, when there was just one lone cloud over the mountain's peak, it would rain that day. I doubt there weren't too many summer mornings that went by when we didn't peer out the window and predict the day's weather.

Sitting back down at the kitchen table, I looked up at the painted plywood square that covered a portion of the kitchen ceiling and smiled. Most of the cowboys who worked here left a memory in the horse they rode, or in the house they lived, or in their name scratched on the barn wall, but Sebastian left his memory in that painted plywood square.

Sebastian was a cowboy from the Cananea Ranch. He told us, chuckling, that he was darker than the rest of *"los Mexicanos"* here because *"Soy un Yaqui"* (I'm a Yaqui). After Beatrice moved back into Nogales, he and his wife, Delfina, lived in the house's basement. On winter mornings, he lit the kitchen and living room fires, filled the wood box when needed before he walked to the barn and began his day.

Delfina did the housework during the day while Sebastian cowboy'd, and the two of them did various chores to maintain the house. During the spring and summer, we'd see their gray heads bobbing up and down in arguments as they fed water from the hose onto the lilac and crepe myrtle bushes and various ground covers, which struggled to survive around the house. It was a constant the-sky-is-blue, no-it-is-gray-relationship and eventually, she'd stomp off to fix dinner for them in the basement's kitchen.

He told me about a *curandera* (healer/shaman) outside of Cananea who took in a snake-bitten eight-year-old child. The boy stayed in her hut, slept close to the fire on the dirt floor, and stared at dried bats hanging from the ceiling. She brewed *Gordo Lobo*, a weed with white fluffy balls on it, and other herbs in water from a nearby spring. *El joven* (the young boy) walked out alive five days later, all swelling gone and fang marks healed over. Tied around his neck was a big garlic head, its dried roots attached, which still pulled strength from the land. *"Las brujas saben"* (the witches know), he said emphatically.

If a horse was severely cut, Sebastian went out in the pasture, picked that same plant, and put the cut-up leaves, stems, and flowers in boiling water. After a few hours, he poured the water over the cut. Within a few days, the animal's proud flesh scabbed over and the infection was gone. He had a myriad of remedies for sick animals; some of them worked and some of them didn't.

During the late 1970s, after a hard summer rain, Mom sent two sons of one of the cowboys to the top floor to check for leaks and asked Sebastian to go along with them. The 8000-square-foot, give or take a few feet, asphalt shingle roof was over an older wood shingle roof, which was over yet another shingle roof. None of the three coverings were doing much good anymore, and a new roof was going to be put on in the fall.

Sebastian said early on he'd never go up to the top floor alone because driving to the house one night, he saw a light coming through the top floor's windows, an area without electricity. The next morning, while he stoked the fire, he announced, *"Hay fantasmas arriba, Señora"* (There are ghosts above). Nothing would convince him it could have been a reflection from his truck's headlights. But this time, since there would be two other people with him, Sebastian had agreed to venture upstairs.

Mom heard their footsteps and bits of conversation as she spoke with Arturo in the big kitchen. The sound of breaking wood followed by plaster and paint chips as they cascaded to the floor woke the dog, who sped to the other side of the kitchen and stood barking frantically.

"OOOOOOhhhh, Díos mío!" (My God!)

Two legs hung from the kitchen ceiling.

Hoots of laughter came from the men above.

"¡Ayudamé, ayudamé!" (Help me, help me!) Sebastian yelled. The more he yelled, the more the guys laughed. Mom and Arturo looked up and backed away from the table.

"El loco Sebastian," (that crazy Sebastian) Arturo said as he shook his head.

The lathe and board floor had been soaked by the leaky roof, and the two young Mexicans didn't want to get too close to Sebastian for fear they'd fall also. Poor ol' Sebastian, his hair now plastered to his neck and sweat pouring down his shirt, was held up by some remaining floorboards laid down in 1898. With his arms spread eagle on the floor to keep from falling fifteen feet, he cussed the young kids out while his legs dangled like the lower half of a puppet.

"Just pull yourself up, Sebastian," Mom said in Spanish.

"*¡No puedo, Señora!*" (I can't!) he yelled back.

The young men found a long board in one of the other rooms, laid it on the floor, kneeled on that, and pulled the older man up as more plaster and more chunks of wood fell on the kitchen's linoleum floor.

"Are you OK, Sebastian?"

A deeply lined dark brown face with chestnut eyes and thick gray hair peered through the floorboards.

"*Sí, Señora,*" he said with a monumental exhalation of breath.

The dog returned to her bed comforted by the sounds of familiar chuckles by younger men, words like "*nunca mas*" (never again) by Sebastian and footsteps through the house onto the back porch.

"Guess there was a leak in the roof, *Señora*?" Arturo said with a grin.

I'd been sitting in the big kitchen for most of the Christmas morning, but the view was so beautiful through the big windows: sunny, no wind, flaxen grass, and blue skies. There were other places in the world, I knew, that were just as beautiful, but they didn't hold forty-odd years of memories for me. The Huachuca Mountains, harsh and dark blue like a maturing bruise, held the world at bay. Only a few people ventured over that road that led down into the Valley. We used to go in those mountains years ago and find our Christmas tree. That was the difference, I told my city friends, between growing up in the city and in the country. Everywhere I looked, memories popped up unexpectedly, good and bad, but they were not tenuous connections. They were ligaments that wrapped around the fibrous make-up of my body and fastened me to the land that supported and fed our ranch world. The land would let go of me easily when I left, without thought, while I, at that moment, could not even imagine not being engulfed in its grasp.

This kitchen was the ranch's center. I supposed that was true with most houses. This kitchen held the conversations of cowboys, bankers, friends, and family. A variety of cowboys came and went through this room. The men from the Cananea Ranch had lived their lives punching cattle and riding horses. Some couldn't read or write, but they could look at a herd, remember which pasture a cow came from, which calf belonged to which cow, and what bull had been with her the year before. Give 'em a list of numbers and their head tally was as good as any calculator. As they aged, some moved back to Mexico while others moved to Tucson.

The cowboys who drank stayed until the liquor interfered with their work. "I had to can that one," I heard Mom say more than once. A few of the wives didn't want to live on an isolated ranch without city electricity and TV reception, and those families moved on. Since I wasn't at the ranch on a daily basis from 1973 through 1993, I missed so much of the ranch's day-to-day life. Some things though were consistent: "just one more rain" or "wonder what the price of beef will be this year" or "that's a hell of a colt, there."

Mom, her glasses on, sat at the dining room table, tallying up expenditures for the accountant, or speaking with cowboys about when to horn-brand the registered bulls, or talking with the farmers about planting or baling hay. If she wasn't in her bedroom, she was doing paperwork in the kitchen.

We did an automatic STOP here for fresh-brewed coffee to help us start the farm pumps at 4:00 a.m. or get out the door to check the first-calf heifers at 1:00 a.m. We removed dinner plates from the kitchen cupboards and set the adults' and kids' tables for holidays. Mom didn't do much cooking, but she made the best ice cream. I saw her at the stove as she stirred the vanilla-flavored cream base in the Farberware double broiler, only looking at the recipe for the ingredients, not the measurements.

My oldest son, Michael, at age four wandered over to the white Servel propane powered refrigerator. He reached up for the metal handle, pulled the door open, and knew he'd find some of Grandma's vanilla custard. He stepped on the bottom inside shelf and the old "icebox," as Mom used to say, swayed first to the front, then back then... food spilled on the floor, wire shelving racks slid out, and the heavy door swung back. The appliance tilted, Michael grabbed a tighter hold on one of the shelves as it tilted up and out, and the 1940s era cold storage unit crashed down on the linoleum floor. The old Servel entombed the boy.

Beatrice, who was on the back porch, heard Mom scream, "MICHAEL!" She saw the woman lift up the refrigerator just enough so he could crawl out of the cavity and then let the refrigerator fall to the ground. The grandmother clasped her grandson against her legs afraid to let him go.

A diorama of our family's timeline was held within the light tan walls. I heard my name called and decided to join my family. Pushing open the kitchen's swinging door, I walked into the living room and looked at my brother, his family, and my son as they sat on the couches. That "elephant-in-the-room" I spoke about earlier? We weren't talking about it either; it was trampling us.

"What's going on in here? Are the kids going to shoot that potato gun?" I asked as I sat next to Charlie, my youngest son. He was only one year older than I was when I married and left the ranch in 1973. That was twenty-four Christmases ago.

Sebastian

An Empty Den

2013. The years are zipping by, but wintertime in Ojo Sarco, a tiny town consisting of a few isolated houses in the northern New Mexico mountains, life is set in first gear. I'm house-sitting for some friends while they are in Texas for these cold months. It's been a good retreat, not much else to do here on the "High Road to Taos" except snowshoe, cross-country ski, hike, write, and read.

It stopped snowing during the night. Morning's quiet, that special quiet that comes when the world, cloaked in white, has settled in comfortably and if it could, it'd be drinking a cup a coffee, too. Leaning against the bed's pillows, coffee cup in hand, I watch dawn's light push through the darkness, birds land on white tree limbs, and tailings of gray clouds head east and set free the blue sky above them. The only other glow is a truck's headlights bobbing along Highway 76, just on the other side of the narrow valley's belly, winding through mountains on to Española and Santa Fe. The rest of the world around me is on hold.

This morning isn't much different from the rare snowy winter mornings at the ranch: Cattle and horses face the eastern horizon; snow covered sacaton stalks stand silent on stretches of milk-white rangeland. In the early years, snow fell more frequently. When we lived at the ranch, a neighbor told us that Mrs. Sheeter, a lady who had lived in Lochiel for most of her life, had a picture from the early 1900s of herself in a horse drawn sleigh. Now if the kids get out early enough, they might have enough time to build a stubby snowman before the snow melts.

Last night coyotes traveled through a field south of the house. Their yelping, squealing, and high pitched short yowls of excitement made me wonder if they had killed something or were just hurrying back to their den.

In the late 1970s, I found a coyote in a trap at the ranch. Sun hadn't been out long—long enough though, for the dew to dribble off the grass but still leave a trace of moisture on the stems. Long enough for me to see cattle make their way out of hills and down canyons and settle in around water tanks but not long enough for me to take off my flannel lined Levi jacket.

I'd taken a few days off from work in California so my sons and I could spend a few vacation days at the ranch. The first morning there, I did what I always did—saddled my horse and went riding.

Mom had contracted a coyote trapper from eastern Arizona, and he'd put out a slew of traps in a few empty pastures. We, along with most of the ranchers in the Valley, had lost a lot of calves that year from coyote kills. Now, and even then, it does not feel good to have done that, but traps were a common practice among ranchers to protect their livestock and livelihood.

My horse, Michael, who was named after my older son, refused to get close. He stopped, that nervous-going-side-to-side-but-not-going-forward type stop. I tied him to a tree's limb and walked a ways to the trap.

This coyote, her brownish coat speckled with gray, exhausted from struggling to get her hind foot out of the steel trap, moved slightly. Sometimes the only sign left in a trap was a severed paw. A few tufts of hide lay strewn on the ground, and some splotches of blood had dried on the steel clamp. I saw her distended teats and wondered about her pups. After eating their fill, females return to their dens, then regurgitate their kill as food for their pups. This female's litter is done for, I thought.

A truck pulled off the county road and bumped over short dry winter grass. The sounds of empty traps and metal tools clanged annoyingly in the truck's bed. I thought, Christ, even the ants are taking cover with all that noise. The trapper walked over to me. We looked at each other briefly.

"Well, we got ourselves another one," he commented and walked back to his pickup.

"Wait 'til I'm over that hill before you shoot her, OK?" I said. "I don't want this horse to dump me when that shot rings out."

The hill didn't block the ZAP as it echoed over the brittle grass and through the cold air. The sound did block out the morning birds' conversations and my horse's footsteps when, at that moment, he shied quickly to the side.

Now, I wonder how many pups died of starvation waiting for their moms that winter at the ranch. But then, I don't know how many calves were eaten or how many cows were killed while calving either.

Maybe I'll see coyote tracks in the snow this morning as I walk with the dog on an old logging trail that cuts through the pine trees. Eventually, it crests up on a ridge with a vista of juniper and ponderosa pine covered hills and narrow valleys of northern New Mexico. There is a spot like this place in Upper 21, a pasture on the ranch's east side. Atop a horse, it is as if you are standing on a relief map looking down on small rocky hills falling into a convergence of gentle valleys extending out like a bay that merges with an open sea of gray sage, caramel hued grass, and prickly poppies with white flower heads.

Riders on either side of the pie-shaped pasture pushing cattle down the hills into small valleys and canyons—that also comes to mind when I stand on the ridge. One by one the animals trickled along; one cow would see another and start trotting to catch up, their calves running behind them with stiff little tails. We'd all end up at a windmill and continue to push the cattle down the small valley. We'd fan out again, pick up any strays, move them into the valley, and come to a stop on top of various hills close to the gate.

If one person was missing, we'd wait until the cowboy appeared. We then descended the hills to the water tank and pushed the wanderers in front of us. Cowboys cut out cows with their babies or any dry cows (cows without calves) or bulls, and we moved the animals to another pasture. The routine never varied much, only if the land needed a rest;

then, we moved the entire herd, closed the gate, and left the pasture to enjoy its solace for a few months.

There used to be some corrals from the "old days" constructed from tree limbs in that pasture. Two vertical tree posts set side by side with six- or eight-inch spaces in between, and each pair spaced every four feet or so. Cut tree limbs were dropped in the middle and all were bound by wire along the vertical posts. I see those corrals in northern New Mexico also. They are solid pens for working cattle and corralling horses. There is no need to buy lumber to build them; the land supplies it all.

Every once in a while, when I'm hiking, I pass a God-only-knows-what-number-generation New Mexican Hispanic man driving his cattle onto summer pasture, land that has had the same surname on the title since the 1700s. *"¡Hola Señor!"* I'll say as he and his horse disappear into the pines. They'll hang on to their land; they've done it for two or three centuries now, just by keeping it simple.

The farm and hills of Mexico

Charlie

Whoosh

When you're the youngest on a ranch, you always get all the "Oh, hell, let the kids do that" kind of jobs. So, without having to be told by the two cowboys in the truck's cab, the six-year-old boy automatically hops down and opens the pasture gate. The 4x4 pulls through, and the driver waits for the boy to get back in the truck's bed. The ranch vehicle bumps along the dirt road causing tools to bang in the bed with unharmonious sounds. A few old cows don't bother to look up, just swish their tails as if saying, "Leave us alone."

At the top of the hill, the trio stop and look at the water tank with moss floating on top of two inches of slimy water. Water bugs seem content resting on the green mattress of muck—apparently happy to cool off in the summer's heat. The men look at the tower then glance at one another, and one says, "Well, guess we better get this windmill fixed."

Silhouettes of windmills on tourist postcards convey a romantic image of the Southwest and cowboys—alone and strong. I doubt these two cowboys find anything romantic about this windmill on this hot July morning in southern Arizona. All it means to them is no water for cattle; it needs to be fixed soon, or they are going to have to move the herd out of the pasture this afternoon. So, they set to work as the boy hands them tools from the pickup.

The young towhead helps out when they need him but mostly wanders around, playing with grasshoppers or looking for baby frogs hidden from the sun in the water tank's black slime. The muddy water smooshes up through the dry, encrusted top layer like brown pigment oozing from an artist's paint tube, and small fingers trail through thick goop. Soon the boy's suntanned skin is splattered with dry muddy spots, and it isn't long before one grasshopper looks just like another and frogs get wise to the commotion and move away. The boy looks around for something else to do.

Kids can be so silent sometimes, just quietly blending into the landscape of a room or yard, or in this case, a pasture. Doesn't make any difference if they are wearing a red size six tee shirt with a surfboard stenciled on the back; big people's eyes float over their surroundings when their minds or bodies are occupied. It is as if adults, absorbed in conversation or horseshoeing or, this time, fixing a twenty-five-foot-tall windmill set on a twelve-foot-square concrete slab, focus solely on the task in front of them. Their thoughts enter a tunnel and then, without knowing why, something triggers their mind. Their heads look up and around and say, "Uh-oh, where's Bobby or Tony or Susie?" At this moment it is, "Hey, where's Charlie?"

"Hey, Charlie, where are you?" one cowboy shouts.

"Up here."

"Where?" he yells out sharply.

"Up."

"Up? Oh my God. Charlie, what the ... what are you doing up there?"

"I don't know."

"David, can you believe this? He must've climbed up when we were at the truck."

"No, los niños, nunca sabes (Kids, you never know)."

"Hey, Charlie, are you OK?"

"Yes. I just climbed up to take a look around. I can see Grandma's house and the horses from here."

"You know, as long as he is up there, he could pull that one bolt out for us. I mean the brake is on, and the fan won't rotate and hit him," the cowboy says to the other.

"Hey, Charlie, see that wood platform right in front of you?"

"Yeah."

"Well, put your foot on that and pull that bolt that's sticking out. It's loose—will ya? Comes off real easy. Do you see what I am talking about?"

"Yeah, I guess, OK."

The men stand at the base of the windmill and look up at the platform and the six-year old who is twenty-five feet above them. Without any hesitation, Charlie puts one foot on the wood platform and then the next one, and in a crouched position, extends his small arm.

CRACK breaks the silence, and a piece of wood and the towheaded boy fall in unison through the air.

Charlie sees the windmill tower's bars pass by him. He feels the air whoosh on his tanned arms. The world outside isn't moving fast in his mind. Grandma's house is still there, in front of him—only far away.

The two men below gasp. Their weathered skins bleach instantly. Helplessness smothers them for a millisecond and immobilizes their mouths as if waiting for the dentist to pull out a back molar. David's arms extend out as he braces himself against the metal crossbars.

PLOP.

The man's knees buckle as the dead weight of a sixty-pound boy falls into his tensed-up outstretched arms. David's right arm falls to his side, as Charlie slides down to the ground, and the man leans against the windmill's crossbars with his chin dropping to his chest. The boy leans against David's leg trying hard not to cry. The two men look at one another, put their calloused hands on the small shoulders, and the boy hears, "You OK?" The three of them are silent for the amount of time it takes a hovering crow to land on the broken platform where its nest used to be.

"Yeah," the boy says with his head bent down as he wipes away a tear, "but I didn't get the bolt."

Charlie walks over to the metal water tank and sits in the dirt.

"Jesus H. Christ, that was close," he heard one of them say.

Taking their hats off and wiping the sweat off their foreheads, the two men let out an audible sigh. After drinking water from a canteen to relieve that sucking-moisture-from-the-mouth reaction to what just happened, they go back to work fixing the windmill.

The boy stays next to the water tank, drawing pictures

in the dirt, waiting so he can go back to Grandma's to get some cookies and lemonade.

Charlie, my son, told me this story as we were sitting in a coffee shop in Boulder, Colorado, in 2006. He was 32.

Thirty Seconds

A promotion and another office transfer caused me to move with my two sons from Concord, Northern California, to Southern California in 1979. It was an easy move to the San Fernando Valley with familiar freeways and childhood memories. The kids had settled into school and joined baseball and soccer. A year had gone by, life was good, but that day, I didn't want to be in California.

My sons walked to school as I drove through Westlake Village and merged with the other cars on the freeway at 7:30 a.m. The morning commute was easy as one car followed another onto Southern California's freeway system much like a slow intravenous drip. All I could think of was, I am just like those old cows going through the chute at the ranch, nose to tail in an undulating line, following the leader and then, STUCK, waiting for something or someone to get out of the way. I glanced at the trees on either side of concrete barriers, and their leaves looked permanently mutated from a natural green hue to a coffee-like stained sage. That morning, polluted blue skies and the general city atmosphere left an irritating scratch on my mind.

I arrived at the office building unable to shake that feeling, that irritation. From my office window, I saw men wearing matching khaki uniforms with MBG LANDSCAPE stitched on their shirts and brown baseball caps. They methodically pushed the machines over architecturally designed hills and occasionally adjusted the canvas sack attached to the machine's side. Not much different from moving a gentle cow herd, I thought, just different equipment. Slow and easy, adjust the pace if they're mama cows and babies, we'd end up at the pasture's gate. Ranch horses knew the work and at times, reliance was placed on the equine's knowledge as the rider thought of other things. Animal sounds, wind blowing, horseshoes pinging on a rock. I wished I was outside speaking Spanish to these California workers.

Ringing phones reined me back into the working world of the high-tech electronics firm, but as soon as the conversation ended my focus returned to the scene outside the window. Fall's splotchy green and yellow leaves had become a carpet around tree trunks, and the Mow Blow and Go Landscapers held large vacuum machines to suck up leaves and grass. The men filled black plastic bags with yellowed and wilted foliage from red flower plants, lime green ferns, and hydrangea bushes. One full bag landed in the truck's empty bed. We were their first customer of the day.

All the organic matter got bagged and thrown away to rot inside the plastic in big landfill pits. I remembered Molly, our family's English bulldog, chasing the wheels as I pushed a wheelbarrow filled with branches from pruned rose, crepe myrtle, and lilac bushes that surrounded the big house. We dumped all that organic material onto exposed-dirt patches in the pasture around the house or layered it in the compost pile behind the back porch. Mom stood on the porch and told me where to dump it. "Don't forget to spread it around. Oh, and take the hose over there and water that plant too, dear, will you?"

The exterior of the office matched all the other office buildings on the street with picture perfect lawns, sparkling windows, light brown stucco finishes, wide steps, and heavy dark-tinted glass doors. Again, my mind went to southern Arizona. Two old adobe houses just east of the river, close to the border, were long abandoned, and the rain and wind slowly made them part of the earth again. A house built on the north end as a cow camp for a cowboy or two, three houses built on the south end for cowboys and their families—not one structure looked like the other.

I also saw the blue Chevy pickup next to a dented white and orange truck, whose bed's wood floorboards saw better days fifteen years before, parked in front of the barn. A weather-beaten, ranch-dented, cow-kicked, '64 one-ton Ford truck defied everyone's thoughts as a driver turned the key and the engine kicked in. Yes, it did start and yes, it did run pretty well. And here outside the floor-to-ceiling glass windows, seven 1980 identical white station wagons, all with a car wash sheen, lined one side of the parking lot.

It was so orderly, everything in its proper place.

At that moment, I wanted to hop in the truck with the workers, smell dirt and fresh cut grass, scrunch old leaves and allow the dry shards to trickle through my fingers and form indiscriminate patterns on the ground. The pull to feel the familiar of the ranch and see open skies was so strong that my life within the four walls with phones, typewriters, and corporate-mandated seminars covered me with a black wave of claustrophobia.

I looked at identical green office panels and the blond wood laminated desk, then at the foliage outside, just five inches away from me, but I was unable to hear or smell anything but office.

Salesmen walked by my office and looked like they just finished reading *Dress for Success*, and I wanted to discard my heels for boots, my dress for Levi's and a flannel shirt and to feel salve on my weather-chapped lips.

Phones rang and secretaries crooned, "Mr. Prevot's office, can I help you?" but I also heard the crackling sound of dried leaves under horse hoofs as they made their way along a river bank.

A vent above me pushed the constant seventy-two degree filtered air downward, but I felt sun's warmth penetrating my bare hands as they held a set of reins.

A scene of grazing range cows with large bellies against a background of prairie grass replaced the framed California coastline pictures that hung on the office wall.

I left the ranch eight years ago, yet yellowed leaves still triggered the thought, "We need to get wood for the fireplaces." I closed my eyes and returned to the grasslands.

In Chino Draw, I was surrounded by fallen dead oak trees, and the ground had a mat of dried leaves covering large swathes of dirt. The annual fall woodcutting was in progress. We parked the '64 Ford truck close to the trees. Soon chain saws sliced through the timber. Old flannel and denim work shirts, already ripped from getting snagged on last winter's logs, soaked up smells of the burning gas and oil mixture used to fuel the saws. As the chainsaws cut through the dead wood, the fluctuating whirr-rrr-ing sounds blocked out all conversation, and our ears became immune to the roar. Fireplace sized logs dropped on the dirt like slices of week-old multi-grained bread as our gloved hands threw dismembered limbs into the truck's bed.

I looked up at Benito, one of the ranch cowboys, as he stacked the logs as they landed on the truck's bed. He put one upon another, row after row. The wood side racks looked as beat up as the truck, and I hoped they didn't fall apart before we got back to the headquarters. Oscar took off his goggles, his eyes peered out and were outlined in sawdust and dirt. The word *raccoon* came to mind.

Every year we melded into an unspoken assembly line during the fall season. People might change but the task was the same. A few hours passed, I opened the wire gate, and the old truck went by me and waited as I closed the gate and got in the cab. We stacked the logs by the headquarters and cowboys' houses. A comfortable feeling covered us as we ate dinner that night and someone said, "Well, that's done."

The constant handshake with nature, the interdependency of land, climate, animals, and humans was so integral to my being that I winced as I looked at the carefully planned green space outside my window. Although nature poked her way into the building by way of potted ficus trees and shiny plant leaves, which received weekly care from plastic spray bottles and a monthly measured fertilized chemical dose, the air conditioned smell triumphed.

"Lisa, they're waiting for you in the conference room."

"Oh . . . yes . . . OK, here I come," and I refocused on the file folder lying on the laminated light oak wood desk. Pushing the chair back, I rose, picked up the manilla folder, smiled at the receptionist as I walked by her desk, and continued on with my day at the office.

Dangerous Nest

We were living at the ranch in 1982 and 1983. I had taken a two year leave of absence from work in California. At the ranch headquarters, tulips and daffodils bloomed, and the vegetable garden was ready to receive some early seedlings. Wind dried snap button shirts; Levi's bleached out just a little more while they swayed on clotheslines under the Arizona sun.

Inside the house, a yellow and white checkered oilcloth covered a square oak table pulling the colors of brown linoleum tiles and rich beige walls together, which created a welcoming space for the ranch's business. The blue Mexican glass filled with yellow daffodils signaled spring had sprung! The redwood door stayed open to the back porch from before sunrise, allowing air movement through the kitchen into the living room.

As the shade's tide started to ebb north from the house, we heard the scuffing of boots on concrete steps that led up to the back porch and soon echoed on the wood porch.

Mom, my brother Bob, and I sat at the kitchen table and looked over at the door.

"*Hola, Raymundo. ¿Qué pasó?*" (What is happening?) Mom asked.

"Three colts are down in Pasture 2, *Señora. Las viboras*" (The snakes). His sixty years of weathered skin looked as if it had aged another ten.

Our three heads dropped in unison as we said, "Oh no."

We drove out in the pasture. It wasn't a pretty sight. Two old geldings stood in the background and looked at the scene before them. Three colts, fourteen to eighteen months old, all weaned from their mamas months ago, stood with their heads hanging down; their breaths rasped through swollen, almost shut nostrils as fever induced sweat dripped down their necks. They huddled together like orphans on a street corner. Bob had called the vet before we left the house, and all we could do was wait, bathe them with cold water from the trough, and try to keep their nostrils open.

Springtime in the Valley brought wind, clear skies, crisp mornings, warm days, and new life. Smoke from fireplaces made its way into the country air before the sun woke up. The fires in wood stoves smoldered during the day, and fresh wood stoked warm embers as the sun said good bye behind the Nogales Mountains.

Dirty-blonde bunch grass lost its strength during wintertime and then in spring, emerging tender green sprigs selfishly sucked ground's moisture. The John Deere tractor grumbled to life at the farm and tilled the fields—up and down, up and down—and only stopped when the plow hit an occasional century old metate giving the driver an opportunity to break up the monotonous work.

Along with all the wonderful aspects of spring, rattlesnakes wake up, begin to wander out of their dirt-tube homes, and stretch out on clay earth looking like thick pieces of rope basking in the sun. Green, brown, and beige mica-like scales on the reptiles' skin sparkle in the light. These curious young colts had poked their heads down in the grasses and WHAM!—fangs had penetrated their muzzles and injected lethal doses of venom into the equines' systems. These colts with soft brown hair, small hooves, and teenage knobby legs had hit the jackpot.

"Must have gotten into a nest of rattlesnakes for all of them to get bit like that."

"Jesus, this is the worst I have ever seen. Poor little ponies."

"Qué triste. Es una lástima" (How sad. It is too bad), Raymundo said softly to no one in particular.

Doc Pickrell's white truck roared down the dirt road and within minutes, the vet set up a triage. He inserted syringes filled with God-knows-what in the colts' bloodstreams, poured coffee mixtures into bags and the young horses received caffeine enemas. Big irrigation lamps set up on tailgates gave us needed light as darkness set in. Colts' breaths sounded like old men's death rattles, and their pulses barely kept up with their hearts' desire to live.

Soon one colt's legs buckled as he fell on the ground and died. The next one didn't last much longer. By 9:00 p.m., only one horse with his nose on the ground and his body against a tree, remained alive.

Ranchers become accustomed to death. Animals die by lightning strikes or graze on poisonous grass or a coyote kills them. Cows give birth to still-born calves, or a horse is shot because of a broken leg. But that night, seeing three young colts bunched up together, all of us knowing their time on earth was only going to be a few more hours—that was tough.

We'd remember them though, after summer bled into fall, when we rode by their bleached carcasses and felt grateful that buzzards, coyotes, and weather had done their job. The black scavengers smell the decay in the air and circle the animal. The bravest of the birds descend and peck one soft shiny spot on the carcass—the eye or stomach. Another flock member swoops down on the ground, totters over to the still body, other birds follow, and the carcass becomes an unrecognizable mass with a blanket of black birds. Dead animals remain on their deathbeds and rejoin the world in a different way. But, with rattlesnake deaths? Sometimes the birds stayed away, I noticed.

Raymundo remained with the colt all night, and the next morning we drove out to the pasture to relieve the "watch." The colt's legs lost their strength during the early hours, but his brown stomach still rose slowly. His eyes opened as I crouched by his body and stroked his head. We swabbed his neck with some water, gave him another coffee enema, and trickled water down his throat from a plastic bottle used to nurse orphan calves. Afternoon came, we headed back to the house and Raymundo stayed. None of us gave the horse much hope.

The next morning Raymundo knocked on the kitchen door.

"Señora, es un milagro. El caballito está en los corrales" (It is a miracle. The colt is in the corrals).

The cowboy had left the horse at 3:00 a.m. for some coffee and breakfast, and when he returned two hours later, he found the horse in the trap (small fenced-in pasture) by the house. The horse had dragged himself up from the pasture during the night, had walked when he could, and had lain down in the mud where some water seeped from the water trough. One of his shoulders looked as if it had been through a meat grinder and was filled with dirt, rocks, and grass stubble. His forelegs were bloodied and cut. His tongue, thick, limp, and gray, hung out the side of his swollen mouth. Big brown eyes stared at us while we held his head up and gave him water.

He stayed down while his body hung on to life, and each rib slowly became another noticeable bone on his young hide. He nickered softly as humans stroked his neck. Rope-scarred and calloused hands moved over the colt's body with a gentleness of having seen undeserved pain. We washed open sores on his shoulder and legs with boiled water steeped in medicinal herbs found in the pastures by the cowboys. One of the old timers, Mrs. Bercich, had given us a jar of lamb's fat with some herbs in it a few years before, and we smeared the goo on exposed proud flesh. Red yarn poked out from some old saddle blankets that served as cushions for his shoulders and hips. If he had another call in the Valley, Doc Pickrell stopped by and gave him a shot of something, walked up to the big house, and told another story about some snake-bit horse he'd seen in his life.

Five days passed and the horse began to look like a horror movie prop. From his mouth came rasping guttural breaths sending ripples of pity though anyone who saw the crippled animal. Vultures waited in the cottonwood trees. Our conversations centered around the questions: Should he be put down, how much longer, what to do? His four legs struggled to regain their memory, their strength, their purpose, moving back and forth making a fan's image in the dirt.

Day five was our D-Day. It was his, too. His head and neck didn't do the then familiar smack on the ground when he tried to lift them up. Rejuvenated cells found solid footing, the rest of his body kicked in, and he finally stood up.

Six months later, he grazed in the pasture along with other horses. Milagro's lower lip hung down like a wet, dirty dishrag sweeping the dirt with each bite. He became another ranch horse with a story.

Cowboys rode the big bay horse with his constant wagging lower lip. When a solid roping horse was needed, they haltered Milagro. His shoulder healed over but always looked like the rough side of a granite outcropping. He lived for another seventeen years until arthritis crippled him so badly that we had to put him down.

That spring shortly after Milagro recuperated from

his snake bite, Sonny, a neighboring rancher, Bob, and I helped Mom down the porch steps and took her to the Patagonia Clinic. With each cough, her handkerchief received fresh blood. Within the hour, she was in an ambulance on her way to the hospital in Tucson.

"Double pneumonia and a lung infection. If she makes it through the night, she should pull through, I think," the doctor said.

I knew she hadn't been feeling well but she still walked to the barn, and I had driven her into town the previous day to do some errands. She kept saying, "I'm fine." But, even if I had tried to get her into the Patagonia Clinic, if she didn't want to do something, a simple "no" on her part always silenced everyone in the room.

The big house echoed for two weeks as she, now seventy-six years old, recovered in the hospital. Oh, cowboys lived in the basement, ranch work still went on, but the core was gone. Mom returned with an oxygen tank for night use only. It was the first time when Ruben and his wife, Carmen, came to the ranch from Mexico.

"**M**om, an officer from Nogales brought a man from across the line to help out in the house. They're outside."

"Well, bring them in, Lees."

The two men followed me into the big kitchen.

"Mrs. Sharp, you asked about finding someone to help you around the house, yard work, and cowboy. I've been buying shrimp from Ruben, now, for a couple of months. He's a good man, Mrs. Sharp, and willing to work out here."

The young Mexican man and the older woman started sizing each other up as they spoke in Spanish.

"Can you milk a cow?"

"*Sí, Señora*, I worked on a dairy farm starting at age thirteen through twenty, six days a week, 4:00 a.m. to 4:00 p.m."

"Can you cowboy?"

"*Sí, Señora*, as a kid I helped on *un ranchito*."

"Can you help keep this house in one piece?"

He didn't understand the phrase "in one piece," looked at his friend, and asked in Spanish, "What does that mean?"

"Can you fix things?"

"Oh, *sí Señora*."

Mom hired Ruben for two weeks to see how they would get along; he'd live in the basement with the other cowboy. After leaving the dairy farm in his late teens, Ruben worked for a Mexican government contractor involved with Mexico's screwworm-fly eradication program. In the early 1970s, he moved to Nogales, Sonora, and drove a Coca-Cola distributor truck. Like a lot of Mexican men during this time, he also crossed the line and worked at ranches and farms from Nogales up to Marana returning to his family every couple of weeks. He told me once he'd been picked up nine times by the same border patrol agents. They all spoke about their families, where there was work, and what was going on in Mexico and the U.S.

Married at age eighteen, now in his early thirties and supporting a family, he decided to start his own small shrimp distribution business after he won a 1978 yellow Renault Le Car in the Mexican lottery. He told me he could run his hand through the sand in Huatabampo, Sonora, where he grew up and lift up a half dozen shrimp. The idea was sealed when he had the winning lottery ticket for a 1979 Le Car, a white one this time, the following year. Business was good in Nogales, but he missed *el campo* (the land/open space).

After a few weeks went by, Mom asked Ruben if his wife could do housekeeping and cook for her. A week later, the couple began to live in one of the two bedrooms in the big house's basement. They worked four days at the ranch and on Thursday nights returned to Nogales in the tiny 1979 white Le Car. Their three daughters lived with Carmen's mother in Nogales. Many years later, Carmen told me how many nights she cried over not having her daughters with her during those first few years at the ranch.

"*¿Puedes poner el vendaje en mi pierna, Carmen?*" Mom asked. (Can you put the bandage on my leg?)

Carmen sat next to Mom's legs, which now had to be bandaged daily to keep the swelling down, and wrapped the elastic band around her calves and ankles. She learned to cook the food that Mom liked from instructions that went like this: "Put a little of this in and some more of that in," or "Don't pay attention to the recipe, Carmen. Let's try it this way."

Bob had put in a bell that connected to the cowboys' room in the basement in case of an emergency. Ruben did house maintenance, stoked the fires in the early mornings, and added "cowboying" to his repertoire of "things I have done in my life." The last job wasn't hard since he'd ridden as a kid in Mexico, cowboy'd on farms and U.S. ranches, but he hadn't done it his entire life. The other cowboys, well, that's all they'd ever done, and Ruben watched and learned.

In 1988, after Mom left for California, Ruben and Carmen moved their family from Nogales to a cowboy house south of the headquarters. A year or so later, their fourth daughter arrived. She was born on Mom's birthday.

Ruben's girls all finished high school. The oldest girl is married with children. One received a degree in International Business, married, and moved to Rhode Island. Another is married, and the couple work in a hair salon in Tucson. The youngest girl is currently attending Pima College. The family received their immigration papers in the early 1990s.

Ruben and Carmen are finishing up their own ranch circle. They live in the house I left on August 17, 1999, the same house my brother and his family lived in until 1990, and the same house where Ramon, one of the first cowboys from the Cananea Ranch to work at San Rafael Ranch, lived in when he started working for *la Patrona* in 1960.

During my last years at the ranch, a group of illegals stopped by in the wintertime, on their way back to Mexico. They were lost and trying to get back home. I had a puppy, who for whatever reason, followed them on down the road after they had drunk some water and left. I soon noticed she was gone when her chubby furry mass wasn't tucked in by the wood stove. I saddled a horse since it was softly snowing, and I couldn't drive out on the muddy roads. I followed their tracks in search of the dog.

On the way, the Border Patrol passed me on the road, and I asked them, "If you see my puppy, can you bring her back to me?" Fifteen minutes later, their Ford Expedition returned with the four illegals in the back. The agent handed the puppy to me through the SUV's window. I put her in between the saddle and my belly, and we returned home. The illegals were processed through the system and released a few days later in Mexico.

I saw a Border Patrol agent from the old days recently, and we spoke about how different times were then. Some of their biggest concerns were looking for the *polleros* (illegals crossing trucks filled with chickens or trucks filled with appliances and used clothing), the illegals who cut the fences and crossed without regard for property or if a crime had been committed. When the Border Patrol picked up the migrants before the late 1990s, the fear of violence erupting wasn't such a prominent issue as it is now. There were maybe two or three Border Patrol agents assigned to the entire Patagonia, Sonoita, and Valley area. They knew all the cowboys and their families and stopped at the farm to ask about what was going on in the area. If they saw us working cattle, we'd stop and talk. If there was an issue, a rancher might say, "Saw something a little suspicious in this area, you might want to check it out." New agents were introduced by those leaving, and we'd sit at the dining room table, drink coffee, and speak about the comings and goings in the valley.

Now there is an official Border Patrol Station in Sonoita with a parking lot is filled with cars, SUVs, and horse trailers. If I drive out to the Valley in the early morning, I will pass seven or eight Border Patrol trucks on their way to patrol the Valley roads and grasslands area.

Nogales mountains in the background; the pasture that Milagro crossed

San Rafael Valley grasslands

Summer

Charcos (small pools of water) filled the land's crevices after a summer rain. On early morning walks or rides, I saw coyotes, deer, antelope, and javelina belly-up to the bar in their neighborhoods. The pastures invited you to dive in and swim across their green waves of sideoats, blue, black, and hairy grama grasses. Humidity infiltrated the hot dry air as voluminous white clouds made their way northeast from Mexico's coast for afternoon rains.

The sun fought battles with dark ash thunderheads that touted their superiority. Arroyo veins, sandy washes, and stream beds filled with summer monsoon rain and turned into a liquid mass and fed the Santa Cruz River. The world settled again, and tentative rays poked around milky pillows as if to say, "Is it safe, now?" Puddles reflected a silent Morse code, and sun gained a foothold between the clouds.

Goddamn it's hot.
Ride at daybreak.

Brand before 9:00 a.m.
Bale the hay in the morning before the rains.
Fence work—non-stop.
Horse flies, mosquitos, red ants, and grasshoppers.
Fat horses, cows and soggy calves, weaning colts.
Keep the oven OFF during the day, please!

Summer monsoon season brought water to the Valley, weight on the calves, and moisture for the summer grass. Smells of moisture and dust-free air surrounded me as I rode my horse through the tall grass. Leaning over the horse's shoulder, I pulled a green stalk from its shoot and sucked on its liquid. I remembered this scene ...

During the early 1980s, some men from across the line hot-wired a truck in the barn during the night and drove off with saddles and other tack. The next morning, we found it stuck axle deep in mud south of the farm with the tack still on the bed. When one of the cowboys heard the tack had been found, he galloped bareback on the ranch stallion past the headquarters. This young man's sole possession was his hand-tooled saddle, and he wasn't going to wait another minute for us to pull the truck out of the mud.

An hour or so later, the contented cowboy, hat pushed back some on his head, rode the tacked-up stallion past the ranch house and on to the barn. What a sight! Sun rays nipped the horse's deep red mane and tail, summer grasses covered the stirrups, set against a backdrop of dollops of cream-colored clouds, which dotted sapphire skies.

Rollin', Rollin', Rollin'

"**C**UT!"

A water spigot of people opened; activity erupted around the headquarters. Every two years or so, a movie crew came down to the ranch, disrupted life but brought their checkbook to us, motels, restaurants, and small service businesses. The ranch was an ideal setting for Western movies: no power lines, a big house for the cattle baron (benevolent or evil), cattle, sheep, cowboys, and large expanses of private land.

One stipulation in our contract was non-negotiable: One designated person from the movie crew handled all communication with Mom. Cows still calved, animals had to be fed, and farm and ranch work needed to get done— animals and weather do not care if there is a movie star in their midst. Our rule was unless it was urgent, do not bother the owner.

In the early 1960s, I was in school in Pasadena, but, since then, having seen enough movie filming over the years, this scene isn't hard to imagine: the people, the pandemonium, the director's irritation when a cow suddenly appears in the background.

The actor walked down the porch stairs.

"Get that bulldog off the porch steps," the director yelled.

"Are you going to ask Mrs. Sharp?"

"No, but somebody needs to tell her to keep the dog inside."

"Not me."

"I'm not."

"Me neither."

"All right. Someone call the dog and give her some food and get her out of the way," and the movie kept rolling along as the film crew members thought, "Well, that'll be edited out."

The assemblage of people, horses, and wagons flowed from the porch out to the pasture. A cowboy waited at the barn, heard "CUT," and walked up to the big house. Onlookers shuffled forward to get a better look at a movie star. Caterers finally found the location manager and said, "Lunch'll be ready by noon." Buckboards, wagons, cowboys with six-guns on their hips, women in gingham dresses and bonnets stood in Pasture 2, just south of the house, waiting for their cue to, once again, move on the word "ACTION." Thick black electrical cords snaked over the Bermuda grass giving power to 500 watt lights on tripods. Small generators vibrated with an irritating sound which added to the general melee when a shot wasn't being filmed. Tall director chairs with stenciled names on the canvas blocked confused red ants in search of their hill and queen.

People scurried around with clipboards and make-up kits, stumbled on unaccustomed ground, and clutched the tools of the trade to their chest. Word had spread quickly that a movie was being filmed at the Sharp Ranch, so onlookers added to the temporary invasion, chaos, and noise.

Amid all this hubbub, Molly, Mom's dog, wandered around on the grass as people gave her a pat and just another little bit for her ample brown body. The dog's Save-the-Children's big brown eyes buckled the resolve of an extra eating his lunch, as he tore one piece off his sandwich and then another. She lay down next to him, her head on his foot.

When the English bulldog puppy arrived, someone looked at her smushed-in nose with folds of skin that scrunched around her eyes and hung down below her jaw and said, "Huh, that dog run into too many parked cars?" Molly followed Mom everywhere, inside and outside the house. When she heard the sound of truck keys and wasn't invited, she walked to the porch's edge, stared at the departing truck, plunked herself on the door mat, and waited for her owner's return.

Food, rolling wheels, and chickens gave the dog incentives to propel herself off the porch or the floor in front of the wood stove. She alerted any available human being in her vicinity when it was breakfast, lunch, and dinner. All of us contended with Molly who tried to bite the wheelbarrow wheels while we worked in the yard or cleaned the horse stalls or corrals. A double hog-wire fence saved the chickens.

Earlier that year, one of the ranch farmers drove a tractor to the orchard and cut all the blackberry bushes, since they probably hadn't been pruned in decades, if ever. Mom went down to check on the progress and took Molly with her. The dog nosed her way through the grass, barked, and ping-ping-ping. A porcupine. An hour or so later, Doc Pickrell on his way to another ranch call, met them at a Nogales gas station, sedated the dog, and pulled quills out of her throat and mouth on the ranch truck's bed. His truck served well as a full service vet clinic, and he saved the dog's life that day. Months later, quills were still working their way out from her mouth and chest.

The dog had her own red leather chair in the hall and contributed to conversation with a whiss-ss-ling sound of air trying to make its way through the bulldog's nose.

Molly

The dog sat on the porch observing all the activity.

"We're going to roll the wagons. Get 'em going from the road by the barn and on down the hill."

"OK people, let's go. Let's get it going within the next fifteen minutes."

The horses stood still and waited for men in heavy brown dungarees to sit next to women in Hollywood-prairie dress on the wagons' buckboards. Rent-A-Cowboys with bored looks on their faces that said "another movie and another paycheck this month" rode their movie-experienced horses. Molly lay down on the porch since no food seemed to be in the horizon.

"ACTION!"

The wagons started to roll. Slowly, slowly the wooden wheels crushed dried grass and pushed pebbles deeper into the soil. Women's bonnets kept the sun out of their eyes as they chatted with menfolk and horses plodded over bunch-grass. Cowboy-clad riders with their six-guns rode along-side the wagons. Sounds of creaking wood and chattering voices floated in the air.

Molly heard the movement, lifted her head, catapulted down the porch steps, and tore across the pasture with her eyes focused on the wagons' wheels. Within a minute, activity came to a halt.

"I didn't see her," a driver said.

The dog's stomach moved with her heart's rhythm as she lay outstretched in the pasture with a wagon wheel two feet from her left side. The crew heard the dog's low whimpers but saw no movement except for her stomach rising and falling.

"Don't move her. Let me take a look," said an older man who was the Animal Humane representative for the film.

"Who is going to tell Mrs. Sharp?" the director asked.

"I am going up to the house now. I'm sure Mrs. Sharp has a vet for this dog. Looks to me like the dog has a broken back," said the animal rep.

"WHAT?" echoed out to the field and the front door slammed. A crew member backed a station wagon up to Molly while a few construction people rigged up a stretcher for the bulldog. Sliding the canvas under her and with a "On the count of three: one, two and three," they lifted her into the back of the car. Mom led the way to Nogales as the station wagon tried to keep up with the dust cloud. Three hours after the accident, the movie company had a plane at the Tucson Airport to transport the dog to Fort Collins' College of Veterinary Medicine in Colorado.

The dog had a broken back.

Two weeks later, Molly appeared with her vertebrae screwed to a plate in her back. Two men from the movie crew carried her up the porch stairs on a stretcher, and she again regained her position as queen on a brand new L.L. Bean dog bed, this time though, in the kitchen. She continued to live an active life until age twelve when she joined the other ranch animals in the Arizona blue skies.

Thirty-plus years had gone by since that movie was filmed. I was back at the ranch and lived at the upper end. I looked down at Athena, my black lab/cross and hoped she enjoyed ranch living. How could she not? It felt so good to be horseback riding every day and not in an office environment. Missed my kids, but Michael worked, and Charlie moved to Boulder for college.

As I rode over the hill in Pasture 7 on my way to the headquarters, I did a double-take at what I saw at the bottom of a hill. A good-sized field of sunflowers that had been carefully grown at the University of Arizona's greenhouse in Tucson lay wilted on the ground. Well, guess that plan didn't work for the film crew, they must not had known that it froze at night in the Valley.

On the other side of the road were two clapboard movie-set houses with white picket fences, rolled-out green turf lawns, and pots filled with geraniums. The houses' front doors opened onto a four-foot wide floor, just enough room for an actor to close the door behind him. If he walked any further, his feet would meet the air and drop onto the ground below.

When the director and producer of *The Fantastiks* first came to the ranch in 1994, they saw the blimp over the Huachuca Mountains. It was part of the Tethered Aerostat Radar System, one of ten blimps set up jointly by the Air Force, U.S. Customs Service, and U.S. Coast Guard to detect air, land, and sea movement along the U.S./Mexico border. During certain hours of the day, a reflection could be detected in the sky and could cause some issues with filming this movie. We were told the blimp had to go, and the movie representatives were going to speak with the Base Commander at Fort Huachuca and ask him to take it down.

At the time, I wondered how that would work out. It didn't; the blimp was still in the sky. It was a dot since its altitude ranged between 15,000 and 25,000 feet. Maybe the sun reflected off it at times. I didn't know, never paid much attention to it, but hoped the crew could work around it.

As I rode past the houses, some of the movie crew drove up to the field. They walked over to the flowers, shook their heads, and I heard a few expletives.

Later that afternoon as I rode back home, the crew told me the director had sent the greens person back to Tucson to locate two hundred sunflower plants with the order, "Make sure they are at least six feet high." They also told me it was going to snow the next day. It was my turn to shake my head. The sky was blue and clear.

Sunflower Mountain with an altitude of just over 4,000 feet, has the highest land elevation in the Sunflower State. Yet behind the two set-houses, which were supposed to be in the plains of Kansas, were the 9,000-foot Huachuca Mountains. If they could make it snow in twenty-four hours, they could probably get rid of those mountains somehow, I imagined.

The next morning, the breakfast truck was at the "Kansas location" with doughnuts, coffee, and fruit, which were more appealing than my usual egg and toast. My mare liked the carrots and apples since they were a rare treat for her and Athena had a nondiscriminatory attitude about all food, we joined the crew members and watched the set-up for the day's shooting.

The crew brought over portable generators from one of the tractor trailers and plugged in portable fans. They unloaded big bags labeled INSTANT POTATOES from a truck, sliced the tops of bags, and scattered the white flakes on the dirt road for one-quarter of a mile.

I got my horse, figured she was going to go ballistic when the generators started and what was going to happen with the four-inch deep dried potato flakes on the road. We walked off the road and stood a good distance from the filming. The boy and girl, bundled up in scarves and plain dark wool jackets, began to walk. The generator started its low roar, fans begun to blow, and millions of tiny instant mashed potato flakes swirled around the two young actors. It was snowing in Arizona in sixty-five degree weather under blue skies.

I had seen corral fences bust apart as trick horses fell on pre-broken fences and houses erected in two days. I'd seen wounded men and dead men get up and walk away as soon as the word "CUT" was in the air, but the dried potato flakes won the prize. Clever. I rode back home and left the snow behind.

New sunflowers came the next day. The crew dug shallow holes with dirt mounded around the black containers and filmed another scene in the afternoon. A fair amount of people left with potted sunflowers that evening. We didn't need any sunflowers since they grew wild along the farm road. I said, "Thanks anyway," and rode home.

After the movie crew left the ranch, I went over to the small empty valley. The film crew had torn down the houses, reseeded the trampled-down pasture area, and picked up all the discarded debris. It seemed so lonely and deserted. Even Athena looked around; she probably wondered what happened to her morning treats.

A few weeks later, we moved cows over the memories of clapboard houses and sunflower fields, and someone said, "Remember when the flowers all froze, that cost 'em some, I imagine." We continued on to the fence gate as our eyes scanned the herd for cows that needed to be culled.

Charlie, Daniel (my nephew), Mom, and me

One Last Time

Thinking back now, I understand why my mother had such terrible panic attacks at the ranch. As the congestive heart failure progressed, it zapped more strength and oxygen from her body like a balloon with a small pinprick. Beginning in 1986, Mom began to leave the ranch frequently to see her doctors in Pasadena, California. When she returned to Arizona—the lack of oxygen, the distance to medical facilities, the solitary life in the house, the inability to think clearly, and her body in decline—the combination of these things equated frustration for the once-independent woman. Cowboys lived in the basement, Bob and his family lived on the ranch's north end, but she was still alone in the house's middle floor.

She moved to California full time in 1988 for medical care. The familiarity with Pasadena, old friends, and doctors eased her worries, but it wasn't home. In June 1990, after she nearly died from a congestive heart failure bout, the doctors' prognosis was not good: They gave her another few months. Family members and physicians decided it was time to return to Arizona. She and I flew on an ambulance plane to Tucson where she went into a rehabilitation/nursing home.

Six weeks later, with a walker in front of her, the eighty-four-year-old woman walked out of the rehab center, and Bob drove her to a rental house in Tubac, a small village south of Tucson. After three years though, full-time nursing care became prohibitively expensive. I moved from Albuquerque to the house on the ranch's upper end in 1993, and she moved from Tubac to live with me that same year.

"In a few days, we're going to move you from Tubac to the ranch, Mom. I moved into the house at the north end. Generator and windmill are working now, a solar battery system has been installed for full-time electricity—we're good to go." She looks up from her wheelchair, a worm-like tube dangles from her face, rests on her lap, and has its mouth attached to the portable oxygen machine. The gray-haired woman sighs and mutters, "OK."

Her gaze returns to the golfers outside the window. Ten years of progressive congestive heart failure, bouts of pneumonia, and pulmonary edema had taken their tolls.

"I'll be back tomorrow morning around ten to pick you up."

I leave after saying goodbye to the caregiver and drive sixty miles back to the ranch.

Walking through the house at the ranch, I check for anything else needed for her care. Obsolete Mexican tiles with hand painted light green birds are inlaid on the kitchen and bathroom counters, and plain wood cupboards line the kitchen's west end. The chest high brick wall dividing the small kitchen area from the dining area was built from old discarded bricks found in the machine shop at the head-quarters. These little touches have added warmth to an otherwise cold house or "cowboy camp," as some called it.

Michael, when he was growing up, spent many summers with his aunt and uncle at this house. Weathered barn wood cut in various lengths and a few display nooks line one wall of the dining area. He told me about pulling out one board on that wall, and inside was a hiding place.

It feels like eons have passed since my brother, who had been co-managing the ranch with Mom since 1975, and his family lived here—so many changes in the past five years. Mom left the big house, and my brother and family moved there. I moved back to New Mexico in 1985, continued to work in Albuquerque until June 1993 when I sold my house and moved to the ranch to help with Mom's care. Mom and I are back where we started in 1958, but now, the roles are reversed.

Looking out the living room's bay window, I remember when I first saw this place. Mom drove up the two-track road rutted from years of cowboys driving trucks over it, checking windmills, and leaving off salt blocks for cattle. One and one-half miles of rocks scraped the car's undercarriage as we went up a hill and followed the ridge.

We should have taken a truck.

It was late summer in 1959. A barren, long concrete building with a tin roof stood before us and looked about as welcoming as the Old Yuma Prison. The surrounding scene wasn't much better; there wasn't a tree to block the wind or the 360-degree views. Dust devils twirled exposed dirt and had free rein on the land as the miniature tornadoes traveled between patches of grass. We heard the windmill, its fan spinning wildly in the paddock below the house. The wind whipped over the low hills, funneled into the low-lying canyon, and swept up the hill and over us. Water pumped up to the storage tank by the house; the overflow tumbled into a twelve-foot square concrete water holding tank surrounded by cedar fence posts wrapped with rusted wire. The posts had long given up the fight with the western wind.

"I wonder if there was a sale on cement during the 1940s, Lees. This entire house is made of concrete."

Four rooms, all in row, each with a door that opened onto a screened-in porch with a concrete floor. The wind grabbed the wood screen door and it banged relentlessly against the wall. For a couple of single cowboys the house was OK, but not for a family, at least that's what Mom said as we walked up to the door that day. She finished her walk through with, "The only thing lacking here is a jailer and key."

The next year, Ramon Carrizosa and his family moved into the house with its new addition, an indoor bathroom. A small propane Servel refrigerator from Ronstadt's Hardware in Tucson stood in the kitchen along with a Sears stove. Birds couldn't fly into the screened-in porch anymore, so they contented themselves with nests around the house. The couple and their son stayed there for a good number of years.

Ramon was an old-time Mexican cowboy from the

Cananea Ranch. With his lanky body astride a big red Roman-nosed horse, he roped calves every time with three swings or less. If a cowboy took more than three swings, he never should've started, he told me once during a branding. He also told me if a man wanted to cowboy at the Cananea Ranch, they'd throw him a dried cowhide and he'd have to plait it and make his own *reata* (rawhide rope). If he couldn't, he wouldn't be hired.

Wild rags, the cowboy neckerchief, flat crown hats, wide brim hats, spur leathers buckled on the inside, some on the outside—it all depended on where you rode. Laws for Cowboys to Abide By, I came to learn, seemed to be different depending on what state, what region, what country they're from.

My first branding was at the corrals below this house. I watched Ramon heel (rope both hind feet with one loop) each calf and drag it close to the fire. One cowboy lifted the calf just under its foreleg and hind leg, plunked it on the ground, and sat astride the calf. Another cowboy held the hind legs while others branded, dehorned, and castrated. After the first few, Ramon handed me the syringe, and I was told to start vaccinating the calves. We never had branding tables. We always did it the old way: branded with irons from a wood-stoked fire and roped the calves. After they branded the last calf, a count was done of the mountain oysters, testicles, hanging over a corral board to confirm the count of the now-steers. We heard Ramon's wife yelling, *"Carrizosa, Carrizosa, lonché"* (lunch), from the house. Chili, beans, and tortillas became the set menu for the years that followed.

Over the years, I watched the branding hierarchy

unfold. Young kids held the hind legs first. As they grew older and stronger, they graduated to holding the head, graduated again to roping or branding or dehorning and finally, castrating. Me, when I was at the ranch during branding time, I stuck to vaccinating and holding the hind legs when needed.

Athena's barking brings me back to reality, and I finish unpacking a box of books onto the built-in bookcase in the living room. After Bob married in 1974, he and his wife moved into the house. As their children got older, Bob added on a living room, master bedroom and bath, laid brick floors, and put in a wood plank ceiling. The master bedroom gets the southern solar gain and since it is easy access to the living room, it'll be Mom's room. It'll all work, I tell myself. I always knew I'd come back here after Charlie started college, but didn't think it would be like this. Things rarely work out as planned, do they? Just like my sister's wedding cake, just keep cutting.

1994—It's springtime. We've had plenty of time to settle into a routine here, which is now called "Lisa's house at the upper end." We were so relieved when my cousin Chris, and his wife Gloria, accepted our offer to live here and help out with Mom's care before they started the fall semester Ph.D. program in Flagstaff. The house is full; we all have our own bedroom and one room for storage.

Mom's bell, a small brass ringer with a wood handle, calls me as I sit at the round Mexican table in the kitchen. It's 6:30

a.m.—right on time. I did a set of stretches when I got up this morning; the same exercises I saw Mom do every morning during my childhood and on through adulthood. It must be ingrained in my subconscious to lift the arms and legs and s-t-r-e-t-c-h. She said it helped with the blood circulation. In my case, I am hoping it will help with the early onset of arthritis. We'll see.

Athena vacuums the floor with her tongue as she leaves the kitchen to say hello to Mom. The dog has traveled with me for seven years now: Santa Fe and Albuquerque, marriage and divorce, my two sons' graduations, and the U-Haul's front seat ready for the next move. Resting her head on Mom's bed, she waits for the now familiar pat from her friend's thin fingers.

By the time I am ready to leave for the day, the morning routine is well on its way. Mom sits in her wheelchair next to the table looking out the living room window. Her glasses and a book of O'Henry short stories are on the table along with breakfast. Three sheep, generational offspring from the original herd in the 1960s, are in a small paddock outside the front yard, and their bleating for hay causes the daily statement, "Shouldn't you go feed the sheep, Lees?"

"Yes, I will, Mom."

"When will you be back?"

"Around four."

"Where are you going today?"

"Down to the headquarters and see what's going on."

I pass her walker leaning against the wall and notice a small cobweb starting to grow on one steel leg and think stay healthy.

"See you later, Chris, Gloria." They take the 7:00 a.m. to 4:00 p.m. shift.

Riding down to the headquarters, I think about those three sheep at the house and all the commotion caused when the original bunch arrived at the ranch. In 1963, Mom went to D.C. and met with Mo Udall, the Arizona U.S. Representative, who helped with the green card (temporary work-visas) for a sheep-herder and the immigration process for the Mexican cowboys at the ranch. Since those days, practicality had culled the sheep herd down to a hundred or so by the 1980s. We all said a silent thank you.

The sheep brought their own U.N. contingency over the years. Before their respective celebrations, Muslims, Jews, and Greeks came to the ranch and killed a lamb in accordance to their traditions. When I lived at the ranch in 1982 and 1983, I tied up one or two lambs more than once, put them in the back of my Toyota hatchback, and hauled them to Tucson for 4-H kids. Now, we are down to three ewes, which is OK, because Mom loves to look at them.

The day moves along. Ruben, Bob, and I push some cattle off the farm and into Pasture 23, and we do some clean-up around the barn. Riding back to the upper end, it is so quiet; a quail covey flies out of the grass and lands in another thick patch of grass, and three mule-deer scamper up a hill in Pasture 7. No cars, nobody on the roads, a jet stream in the sky, silent days in the Valley. A-OK by me.

It's early evening time and from the living room, we can see the horses grazing the weeds down in the yard: easy, effective, sometimes messy, but it works. The small chestnut filly from an offspring of an RO mare is eating the first spring weeds by the elm tree.

"Reminds me of the little mare I had in Seligman, Lees. Nobody liked to ride the mares, but mine, she took me everywhere," says Mom.

I mention one of the windmills stopped pumping, and we begin talking about putting in dirt tanks to help with soil erosion during the 1960s and 1970s, which led to talking about the road.

"Remember the road grader, Lees?"

"Yes, I do, Mom. You'd see Jack Turner coming down the hill in Pasture 4, tell me to go tell him to stop. I'd have to go out there and ask him to stop grading the road down to the headquarters. You always said, 'The wider the road, the more traffic, and the less grass—the worse the erosion will be on that hill.' He told me once, 'When I saw that truck come barreling up the road, I knew it was either Mrs. Sharp, you, or one of your sisters, even the maid once, gonna tell me to just grade to the top of the hill, don't go down to the big house, and stop going off on the sides.'"

"Poor ol' Jack."

"He was more than a little nervous of you, Mom, and eventually just plain stopped doing that particular road unless it rained."

I finish reading aloud *Death Comes for the Archbishop*, and she tells me it is the little things that keep her going: listening to the birds sing, watching the clouds, and drinking a good cup of coffee.

"Lees?"

"Yes?"

"Did you bring hay up here from the farm today?"

"I got some for my horses, Mom. It's beautiful leafy alfalfa. The smell and freshness of it—you can feel the protein in it. Horses are going to love it."

"What's happening at the farm?"

"It's not like it used to be, just a couple of fields are planted now, permanent pasture south of the road, and a couple of fields of alfalfa by the hay barn. It all costs so much."

I take her to her bedroom and close the house up for the evening. Everything feels as if it is in decline.

Easter time is here. Windy. Up on this hill, we all feel like we're going to end up in Oz shaking hands with Dorothy and the Tin Man.

"Are the kids going to make it down for Easter?"

"Both of them are working and won't be able to get away. When I was a kid, Mom, do you remember the Easter egg hunt at the Pioneer Hotel in Tucson?"

"No. Tell me about it."

The two of us sit in the living room watching the limbs of the elm tree whip back and forth with the spring wind as I reminisce about that Easter Sunday back in the early 1950s. We didn't get to the airport in time to make our plane, so we spent the night at the Pioneer Hotel in downtown Tucson. Bellboys took the luggage as Mom checked us in at the long, carved wood registration counter. The next morning was Easter Sunday, and she wanted to have coffee on the hotel's sun-deck. She had asked the hotel's kitchen staff for some hard-boiled eggs, and they had dyed them for her. I found red and pink and green eggs hidden in the porch swing, in the potted plants, in the terrace's corners—even in the bread basket. The stewardess on American Airlines gave me a second look when we boarded the plane as I carried a blue wicker basket with jelly beans, chocolate rabbits wrapped in pink cellophane, and a package of Viceroys because Mom couldn't get them to fit in her purse.

Eight months have gone by since Mom moved back to the ranch.

"We had good rains this summer," I think, as I wave good bye to Chris and Gloria. They leave pulling their horse trailer behind them and will start school sometime in August. Athena follows them down the road, eventually gives up, and returns to the shade under the apple tree.

"It wasn't supposed to be this way, Lees. I'm stuck. You're stuck. Take me to bed. I need to go to sleep."

I wheel her into her bedroom and go to bed too. Some days we talk with each other, and some days we talk at each other. Some days we don't hear ourselves or listen to one another. Some days are good, and some days we both are in jail.

A few other caretakers come to the house, but "too far," "too lonely," "nothing to do," or "Lees, get rid of that one." A relative of someone from Lochiel is helping now, and maybe she'll work out. I hope. Mom hasn't been able to walk or stand for months now.

"Maria, I'm going down to the headquarters. I'll be back by 4:00 p.m."

I wave goodbye as I ride past the living room window, see Athena jump on the window seat and curl up. The day goes by quickly with cattle work, and I start the ride back on my mare, Pressy. She's young and green but willing and fun to ride. Dismounting at a cattle guard, I open a wire gate, lead her through, and stop to look at the big house in the distance.

My brother's family made small changes in the big house. They tore out the little kitchen and converted it to another bedroom, rearranged the furniture, and did some other things. They needed to make it their home, and a different feeling seeped into the house. It isn't my home anymore. The house at the north end has become my house now, but the big house still grips my heart.

I put my foot in the stirrup, swing my leg over, and feel the little red chestnut mare bunch up and . . . I wake up on the ground. Pressy grazes in the distance with only one rein hanging from the bridle. What happened? I should've tucked her head in to her shoulder, but I didn't. I wasn't thinking. She bucked hard; I flew. I was probably out for a while if she's over there grazing. Well, hell.

I can't seem to push up with my left arm. I get up on the right side feeling my left shoulder just sorta sink, for lack of a better description. I walk over to the mare, readjust the bridle, lead her to the gate, and think I'll unsaddle her and put her in the pony trap. After that, guess I'll just walk to the headquarters.

The ranch truck comes down the hill and stops in front of me.

"Hey, I think I busted my shoulder or something. Give me a ride to the house so I can drive into town."

My nephew looks at me as if I'm nuts; my brother drives me to the Tucson hospital.

"Ms. Sharp, you can't lift anything or take your arm out of the sling for at least eight weeks. It's going to heal crooked and shorten that left side because of the break. We can't cast broken collar bones. You also may have a concussion. Stay here for the night for observation. You need to stay in bed," the doctor says.

He leaves, the nurse leaves, and I get up off the hospital bed in the emergency room and walk out. They have my billing information. My brother and I drive back to the ranch in silence. All I could think of was what are we going to do now?

"Lisa, I have to go back to my family in Santa Cruz. My brother is coming to pick me up tomorrow," and Maria leaves the next day.

"**M**om, you'll be OK here. I can't lift you. We'll come and see you."

"Get out. Go back to Albuquerque."

"Don't come back for two weeks," the nursing home director and the hospice coordinator tell my brother, sister, and me. "It takes that amount of time for our guests to become accustomed to their surroundings."

That word "accustomed" isn't ever going to happen. My sister and I hold on to one another as we walk past a large steel button labeled PUSH FOR WHEELCHAIRS and through the electric double doors to the paved parking lot.

Mom

A Butterfly Flies

After twenty miles of dirt roads and sixty-five miles of paved roads, I arrive at the parking lot in Tucson. I lean my head on the truck's steering wheel, overtaken by guilt when I think of Mom in a nursing home. The familiar chest tightening, then teeth clenching, then jaw locking stops the tears. I pull the truck between two white parking lines.

Walking up the footpath, I look at the two-story pastel pink building and want to find a graffiti artist and say "Here are four walls—go for it."

I want to scream into the air like Johnny Cash singing "A Boy Named Sue", "When I have a son, I think I am gonna name him/ Bill or George! Anything but Sue!/ Anyplace but a nursing home."

Double-paned glass doors open and a blue-haired receptionist acknowledges me with a soft "Hello, Lisa," and continues doing paperwork. The plastic mauve/fuchsia/ lime green flowered upholstery and matching drapes in the reception area show a corporate decorator's hand at work. Signs on bulletin boards line the walls:

ELDERLY PEOPLE HAVE RIGHTS / ACTIVITIES FOR THE MONTH / MENU FOR THIS MONTH. FEBRUARY 1995 is written in big red letters on one white board hanging on the corridor's wall. The calendar displays all the daily activities: crafting, language lessons, Sunday service, Valentine's Day.

Arriving at the nurses' station and nodding at the day nurse, I turn the corner and see Mr. Benson. He lifts his milky eyes, automatically tips his sweat-stained Stetson, and continues shuffling his feet back and forth as if trying to get back out to the corrals.

Mrs. Reilly is standing next to him. "Where are you Francis? Where are you Francis?" comes out of her mouth nonstop. I smile at Mrs. Smelzer, who is in the hall this afternoon, as she says, "Hello Lisa. My husband was in the cavalry, dear, and I was a trick rider. It is easier on everyone if I am here."

"I know, Mrs. Smelzer. Glad you are up and about today," and I keep walking to Mom's room.

Kathy, Mom's day nurse, walks by and says, "Hi Lisa, must be Sunday. You know we just love your mom. She just tells us all to go to hell and to get out of her room sometimes. I hope I am as crusty as she is when I'm eighty-eight." And I think, I'll bet Mom wishes you and your patronizing saccharin Southern-belle drawl go to hell before that.

Butterfly covered wallpaper, a mauve plastic covered chair, and a three drawer compact chest of drawers decorate the room. Mom, her eyes closed, lies on the bed with an oxygen tube pumping life into her lungs. When we moved her here a few months ago, I brought a pottery angel her goddaughter had made and a painting from Mom's bedroom at the ranch and hung them on the wall opposite her bed. Her once five-foot-nine-inch frame has shrunk to five feet five; lifeless gray hair covers her head; swollen legs, ankles, and feet reflect a weakening heart.

The only thing that remains the same are her hands. The thin hands that defied skin cancer, that held two tiny babies from two pregnancies who died in infancy before the four of us came along are still elegant with thin fingers and pale skin. Hands that held the reins of horses and gracefully touched piano keys now lie still on top of the white cotton blanket. As I touch her fingers, my body remembers the feel of the back of her hand, soft and gentle on my forehead when I was sick as a child. I hear, "Let me see if you have a temp, Lees," as clearly as I did when I was five.

"Hey, Mom."

"Hello, Lees."

"I brought a new Tony Hillerman book today. We got some rain last night, light spring rain at the ranch. Brought up some beef broth. Bob butchered a cow. Anyway, thought you'd like some good soup."

"Oh, no, not now. Thank you though," and her eyes close.

She isn't eating much anymore and stopped taking all medication a month before. She isn't going to last much longer, I think. But then, the doctors told us two years ago she would probably only live a month or two. As she dozes, I look at the inlaid silver cross she bought in Venice in the 1930s. On that trip, she'd had a miscarriage in Vienna and while recuperating, she told me, one of the most frightening things she ever saw in her life was watching the Hitler Youth Organization, *Hitlerjugend*, marching down the streets.

During the mid-1920s, she attended McGill University in Canada, and after a year of freezing cold weather, she wanted to go back to the States. She boarded a train and left for San Francisco. While she was there, she bought a bootlegger's roadster that had running boards on both sides of the car for the body guards to stand on as he drove to the "joints." She also applied to Stanford and was accepted; no reference was ever made to McGill University, only that the previous year was "a year of travel." During the summers, she went home to Cananea, where she met my father, who was working for her family's cattle operation, the Greene Cattle Company.

Once when Mom visited me in Albuquerque, I fixed rabbit stew for us, and she said, "I swore when I left McGill, I'd never eat another damn piece of rabbit meat again." We went out for dinner that night.

I think we would have been great friends when she was young. I wish I had known this woman as more than "just my mom."

Sometimes, when I am at the big house, I expect to see her walking out her bedroom's door onto the front porch and say, "Now who's driving up here?" When a tourist got out of the car and yelled, "Hello, can you tell me how to get back to Patagonia?" Mom muttered, "Oh Christ," as the person walked closer. She gave him directions, and the lost soul wanted to hear more about the house: "What's it doing out here?", "It's so big," and on and on. One person asked if we sold tickets so he and his family could have a tour. Most of the time, she didn't need to say, "Lees, can you help this person?" Usually, as soon as I saw an unfamiliar vehicle driving up the driveway, I was already on my way out the door to answer questions or give directions.

The big house invited questions. It summoned people driving by to take pictures. More often than not, the tourists probably said to one another, "Oh, let's see if anyone is there," and we'd hear a knock on the door. Same questions and same answers.

I start reading out loud to her. Thirty minutes pass and I pause to have a sip of water.

"Aren't you going to read anymore?"

"Yes, I'm just drinking some water," and continue to read.

Sundays and Wednesdays are my visiting days. Mom's godchild, Dinah, and her husband visit every week. Hospice volunteers come every day and read. I look at the visitor log, and she isn't alone all the time, but she doesn't belong here. She belongs walking through the fields of alfalfa to see if they are ready for the first cutting; she belongs in the corrals weighing the bulls for weight gain records; she belongs in the hall of the big house calling me on the phone saying, "Lees, can't you get off work, bring the kids, and come down for a while?"

It used to drive me crazy, the phone calls "When can you come back down?" Now I miss them. Once during the summer, I flew to Phoenix from California on business and took Charlie with me. Michael was at the ranch already for the summer. Mom had chartered a small plane for us to fly to the ranch that afternoon.

The pilot was a Vietnam vet, and we dodged the huge

voluminous monsoon clouds as if we were playing Dodge ball on the playground. When we weren't turning, we were dropping like lead in water because of the air currents. We arrived at the ranch, but couldn't land because the cows were grazing on the pasture area. He buzzed the house and soon, the green Dodge truck left the house, drove into the pasture, and began to honk. All the cows, upon hearing the honk, the sound that signaled HAY, followed the truck into the oak trees.

We landed in the pasture; no, we bumped along in the pasture and stopped at the fence line. Michael, at age nine, pulled the truck alongside of us and said, "Hey, Mom, want a ride?"

As I read, I am brought back to reality in a way that only a mother can do, "Lees, I can't believe at your age you still don't pronounce some words correctly. E-pit-o-me, epitome, Lees." At age forty-five, that child in me automatically surfaces and instant irritation bubbles. But it doesn't stay. I don't say anything. Why? I flash to *Beowulf* and my ignorance about the epic poem when she asked me about it years ago. Mothers. Still, I do pay more attention to content and authors' names now. The sun begins to go down, and I have a two hour drive in front of me back to the ranch. I put the book on the table by her bed and look at her. I feel she had been looking at me for a while and ask, "Hey Mom, remember our first night at the ranch?"

"No."

"I do. I don't remember which manager was living in the house in 1960. Summers of 1958 and '59, we stayed at the newly built El Dorado Hotel in Nogales and drove over the Nogales mountains to the ranch. But in 1960, we slept in the bedrooms on the south side and cooked our first meal in the little kitchen. Remember? You heated up frozen peas and cooked some ground beef in a cast iron frying pan you found in those white-enameled metal cupboards. We slept in the gray twin beds along with the flying ants and mosquitoes that came in through the holes in the window screens. We had picked up some citronella candles at Escalada's in Nogales and lit them hoping the smell would keep them away. Didn't help. And you got a broom and swept out the dead bugs and dirt in the bathroom. All the lights went out because the ranch manager turned off the Kohler generator. What was his name?"

"I don't remember."

"I don't remember who was living there either, but we shared the house with them the third summer we went there from California. We'd taken the train from Pasadena, and I kept thinking about our carpeted dining room at home. Where would we all sit for dinner if we lived in this house and only had the little kitchen? I didn't know we were going to get the whole house."

She falls asleep during that sentence, and I think about a statement I had heard years ago, "She must rattle around in that great big ol' house, all alone up there on the hill." Nope, neither house nor woman dwarfed the other. They complemented one another in their determination and willpower to remain on the land.

For the first time in my life, I realize she could have kept the ranch manager on in 1958, stayed in Pasadena, lived her life raising four children, and studied music composition.

Some ranch owners visited their ranch on an occasional basis and lived someplace else. Instead, she moved into the cattleman's world in an isolated part of Arizona and operated a ranch and farming operation. But then, it was in her blood. She'd been raised and lived in the world of livestock and land. It was in her pores and embedded in her soul. And here I am, another woman, thinking about the "glass ceiling" and the corporate world. She probably never even thought of the obstacles she faced as a divorced Catholic woman in those years. At least she never said anything to me about it.

I need to leave and drive home.

"Love you, Mom." I lean over and give her pallid skin a kiss.

Today is Wednesday. She asks me how is Albuquerque, and how was the drive. It's been two years since I was in New Mexico. I wish my mom would come back to me.

The phone rings at 3:33 a.m.

"Lisa?"

"Yes?"

"Your mother died a few minutes ago. She had her rosary in her hand. It was a peaceful death."

It is Sunday, Mother's Day, May 14, 1995.

Mom, family album

A Cananea cowboy

Sebastian, Pancho, and Ramon

Chito and Cananea cowboys

Healing Together

The sun caught Ty's muscle definition on his shoulders and legs as his burnt-copper hide sparkled like tiny Christmas lights glistening in the distance. The shiny black tail, forelock, and mane advertised his adaptation to ranch living—a tall, now muscular body combined with Arab refinement.

The initial pecking order of the horses had changed also. He boasted his athleticism consistent with the Polish Arab breed as he led the horses to the corrals for morning feed. With his head back and tail in a line, he galloped full speed to the barn, flew over the arroyo, spun around at the fence, and waited for the other horses. They soon caught up and stopped behind him.

Walking down the hill from the house, I looked at the bay horse and thought, damn, he looks good!

Head down, belly full with alfalfa, his left hind foot bent and resting, lead rope looped loosely over the rail, the horse waited patiently for me to finish saddling so we could be on our way for a day of checking fences and cattle.

Ty's long tail made a line through the moisture on the low growing prairie grass as we jogged along a cow trail. Winter rains were good and tips of green grass had started to poke up.

Along with spring shoots, gophers and ground squirrels emerged from their underground burrows; coyotes, squirrels, and snakes ventured out for longer periods of time to catch their breakfast and soak up the sun. Bees started pollinating the garden's four apple trees, and cowbirds picked bugs off cows' backs. It was a nice morning, clear blue skies, air felt fresh, smells of morning dew moisture on the grass—life was good.

We loped up a hill surrounding a dirt water tank. Two migrating blue herons stood on the banks, looked at us for a second, and took off with wings flapping as water dripped off their bellies. Both the herons and I took flight; Ty spun a full circle, unseated me, and I rolled down the hill. He stood still, looked at the birds above him, then at me on the ground. He slowly walked down the embankment, waited for me to get up, and get a move on.

Dusting dirt off my Levi jacket and readjusting my hat, I mounted up and continued our ride. Lesson learned again and again: Complacency was not on the dance card.

The sun's rays were in full throttle now, and I figured it must be around eight o'clock. My fingers flicked some remaining dried grass off my Levi's and I thought how lucky this horse's life turned out for him, considering his past, and how I ended up with an Arab in quarter horse country.

In 1995 after Mom's death, I left the ranch and worked for a nonprofit group in Albuquerque. It was an easy place to escape to since my son and some old friends lived there. There I met Rick, a horse trainer, and began to ride horses at his barn, which is where I met Ty.

Ty's lip hung down some, and his tongue looked as if it had been through a meat grinder. I asked Rick about it, and he told me the horse's history. Because his neck didn't do the classic "Arab arc"—a crescent moon shape—the previous owner tried many things to "fix" it.

His tongue and lower lip told the story of the bicycle chain looped through his mouth and attached to a breast collar, which wrapped around his chest with either end buckled to the saddle for stability and constant pressure. His large frame wouldn't conform to the trainer's wishes, and the horse's hide bore the marks to prove it. He learned to flip over backwards, tossing his former trainer in the air to get some peace out of life. The horse landed a few too many times on his left side and buggered up his left hip, which prevented full extension of his left hind leg.

The final straw for both horse and trainer came when Ty, with hoofs and teeth bared, decided enough was enough and lunged at the trainer. The gelding was in the lineup at the next Tuesday's auction block for horse meat. Rick knew some good pedigreed Arabs came out of Ty's barn and went to Tuesday's sale. Instead of in the back of a big semi truck with the other no longer useful or wanted horses, Ty loaded on Rick's horse trailer and traveled to his training facility in Placitas, a few miles north of Albuquerque,

For the first few days, a pen held the 16-hands tall bay gelding in its eighty-foot fenced-in circle while Rick sat on the railing talking to him about life and whatever else came into his mind. On the third day, the Polish Arab looked expectantly at the man as he brought the daily morning feed. Rick walked into the pen and leaned on the fence, the heel of his cowboy boot hooked over the lower rail, elbows rested on a higher rail, and looked like a postcard photo of a cowboy just "hangin' out." The horse ate his breakfast but never took his eyes off the blond-haired man with the black hat, red and blue plaid shirt, and Levi's.

The dance went on for a few more days, and each session was longer than the previous one. Rick added new steps: walking towards the horse, backing away, advancing a little closer, walking to the left then to the right, occasionally turning his back, no constant eye-to-eye contact. He gave no sign of a predator in the form of a human being. He started to touch the horse's shoulder. Next day, his neck and back, next day, his legs, and on and on it went, day after day. A month passed, and the trust scale rose between the two of them, and finally Rick put a saddle on the four-year-old's back.

"Slow and easy wins the race" summed up Rick's training motto. Over the next two years, Rick rode Ty while schooling and ponying young colts in the round pen and arena. If colts got too close to Ty's flank, he'd give them a little kick, just enough to say, "Get off my butt." If a colt thought he was pretty hot stuff, he'd end up in the corral with Ty to be taught some manners. Ty still wouldn't get into a completely enclosed stall or horse trailer unless it was open sided and daylight could shine through. That was the only residue he carried with him by the time I came along. Well, that and "Think twice before you put a bit in my mouth." Rick only rode him with a soft rope hackamore.

I heard the story, looked at the Polish Arab, fell in love with the brown eyes set wide apart and partially covered by his black forelock, and his head held high with a new found confidence that happens when life gives back comfort and security. Over the months, I rode horses in the barn for training, and every afternoon, Ty and I got to know each other on forest trails surrounding the property.

I was sitting at Rick and Gene's breakfast table on an April morning when Rick offered to sell the six-year-old horse to me and haul him to the ranch. Rick and his wife wanted Ty to go to a good home; they needed the money. Eleven months had gone by since Mom's death, and I was ready to return home.

Rick unloaded Ty at the ranch corrals, stroked his furry neck, and handed me the halter as he said, "Take good care of him, Lisa." The next day, Rick left with that empty horse trailer rattling behind him. I imagine it must have been a lonely long drive to Albuquerque that day.

Slowly I settled back into the empty house on the north end. So many memories of caring for Mom before her death hit my face in every room. I could see her sitting in her wheelchair by the table in the living room looking out the window at the sky and ranch land. A forgotten oxygen tank with its plastic tubing attached to the outlet leaned against the wall. One lone prescription bottle, its expiration date long since passed, stood silhouetted against the old fashion four pane wood window in the kitchen. I felt as if I was on a raft floating in the sea and no shoreline in sight.

And Ty? He paced the corrals waiting for his old friend to show up and take him home. The horse and I were a lonesome pair those first few days; both of us had to learn a new life pattern.

Two days after returning home, I rode four miles south to the main house and brought back two older ranch horses to teach Ty about ranch living—wire fences, good grazing areas, water holes, cattle guards—and give him some company. After the horses established the initial getting-to-know-you pecking order, I opened the gate to an adjoining pen, and Ty bolted out as if he was running the Belmont. The one acre pen presented a taste of freedom he had never before experienced. All six years of his life, he had lived in stalls or twelve-foot square paddocks. The ranch quarter horses looked at him as he sped around the paddock. If they could, I wondered if they would've said, "Save that energy, boy. Do you even know what kind of hours you are going to be putting in here? Cow sense is what you need, not crazy stuff."

I rode him inside the corrals with other untethered horses in the pen. We took long rides through open pastures, up and down hills and canyons, loped on sandy river bottoms, and followed cow trails in the country's silence. I had heard cowboys say, "Nothing settles a horse like a wet saddle blanket," and it proved true with this six-year old. Finally the 650 acre pasture in front of the house felt the pounding of three sets of horses' hoofs on pebbles, bunch grass, and cow trails. Ty's education took on another level of ranch life—grazing at will and real freedom.

Dawn brought the sounds of horses running over the land, each horse striving to be first in line. Misty nostrils greeted me as I gave them grain and green hay. I rode every morning, and Ty started to learn about cattle and their wayward inclinations. His first glimpse of a cow about put me in orbit when he stopped but I hung on while he danced and snorted in full anticipation of a frontal attack. We took a step toward the cow and a few steps back. Pretty soon, she got bored and started walking away; we followed. Slow and easy...

My brother and I had spoken early in the morning. Farm work was on the agenda for him, so I decided to take a long ride on the nice spring day. It didn't start out too well, but we were on the trail again. From a hill, I saw the propane truck and knew the tank would be full when I returned home. Now if the wind would just start blowing for a few days, get the windmill pumping, I'd have enough water in the tank so I wouldn't have to turn on the pump jack. When Mom was there, I had learned: turn on the washing machine only when the wind blew.

We trotted along, both of us enjoying the day. I thought about people's reactions when they found out Ty was an Arab. Because of his height, body structure, and straight face, most people didn't know they were looking at an Arab when they first saw him. But the curve of his tail from its base gave his heritage away. Our family's ranch was in quarter horse country. I utilized the Don't Ask, Don't Tell Policy, and it worked well and saved a lot of comments, but when asked, "What's the breeding on that horse?" I didn't blink when I answered, "Polish Arab."

"An A-rab. Huh, Lisa," was the most common reaction from most of my friends and neighbors. As in most country areas, word traveled fast and soon, word got out.

"Her grandfather is rolling in his grave now with a damn A-rab on that ranch. On an RO spread. Damn, it's a break in tradition."

"What'cha want me to shoe him with? Titanium or platinum?" the horseshoer said.

"God-damn A-rabs. Sure ain't good for much 'cept prancin'," was the general feeling about these fine-boned endurance-tested horses.

Ruben, Bob, his sons, my cousins, and I rode and worked cattle, moving them to different pastures for better water or feed, weaning calves, branding, or letting the pasture rest. Occasionally outside help came in for round-up at fall shipping time. Ty and I, a familiar sight on the ranch, jogged to the farthest point of the pasture for the gathers and moved the cattle to the designated meeting point without a trace of sweat on his hide. He loved to cut a cow back into the herd to show who was boss. Our mutual trust level grew, and I relied on him more and more to spot a distant cow or pick his own way down the hills.

Ty shied to the right and trotted quickly away as I tightened up the reins some. What's going on? I turned him around and wanted to get back on the trail. He would not move. So we stood, his ears straight up and forward, every muscle tight, head high and tense, and then I felt in the air the reverberation that went along with memories of two dead young colts, my young mare and her colt.

I dismounted and held on to Ty's five-foot lead rope, picked up a good-size rock, and slowly walked toward the sound. I saw it; a Mojave rattlesnake, light green scales, curled and ready to strike. Any mercy for this creature passed rapidly out of my mind. Eons would go by before these snakes would ever reach the endangered species list, in fact, they were designated as "LC"—least concern because of their large population. Experts said the toxin released was considered the most debilitating and potentially deadly of all North American snakes. The female gave birth to eight or more snakes at a time. So many animals have been sacrificed to their bite. A vet came out and gave whatever concoction of stuff he could and hoped it took; if it did work, sometimes the animal was left gimpy or weakened for life.

The nonstop sh-sh-tk-tk sound hit my ears and revved up the fear factor, but I lifted my arm and took aim. With Ty's lead rope hanging loosely over my arm, I slammed that rock down with all my strength. Ty's head went up with the hurling rock, and he backtracked and stood stock still staring at me.

The first rock hit the snake square on the base of its neck, and it writhed just enough to show some damage had been done but not enough. The reptile retreated back into a coil, and only its head and tongue darted towards me. Looking around, I saw another big rock, said to Ty, "Whoa," as if it would do any good, aimed it squarely at the snake's head, and thought, "I had better hit it or it will come my way." With more rocks, I bombarded the animal again and again, until the snake was a mound of rocks, entrails, and blood.

By the time I was done, only the rattle remained intact. I severed the rattle easily from the dead reptile with my pocket knife. Four good-size interlocked hollow buttons were on the tail, and they would set next to the other two, both from Mojaves, on the tack room's window ledge. There was something sick about keeping those tails, spoils of war, I supposed.

I stroked the bay's horse shoulder, ran my finger over his scarred lower lip, and murmured, "Guess we need to keep on going, Ty, see if the pump jack is still pumping water at the north end of this pasture, enjoy the rest of the morning, and then head home. OK?"

Ty and I, family album

Always a Kid

"You have got to be kidding me, Lisa. Two A-rabs?" I heard more than a few times after Spud arrived at the upper house corrals in 1996.

The flea-bitten gray Arab stood with neck arched and nose tucked in as if waiting for a photo op. His long white and gray speckled tail and mane caught the sunlight's beam. The classic Egyptian Arab dish face and arced tail evoked romantic tales of Lawrence of Arabia or Saladin riding across the desert defeating the twelfth century Crusaders in Jordan. His small dark hoofs, perfect for running lightly across the pastures to gather cattle and head them to the corral or gate, were tough and fanned out in nice compact semi-circles. Problem was, he was an Arab and nobody in southern Arizona's San Rafael Valley rode Arabs for ranch work or for anything else.

"Damn tourists unload their backyard horses on forest lands and leave the gates open. Riding gaited horses or those high tailed prancin' A-rabs—hell, what good is that—the only gaits I need are walk, trot, and lope, and pay attention

137

to the cows," one rancher said to another. Each one had an arm resting on the rolled down pickup window and a wrist hanging over the steering wheel of a 4x4 truck, blocking all traffic on the dirt road.

The term traffic was relative, of course; two trucks might travel on the road in a morning's time. They stopped, and sometimes the driver got out, walked up, and said with a smile, "What the hell's goin' on here?" and probably joined the conversation for a bit before they all went on their way.

Ty blended in more with the ranch horses because of his dark brown coat and black mane, large bones, and straight face. From a distance he was just another tall bay and close up, well, there was something different about him but nothing to comment about. Spud, though, might as well have had revolving neon lights on him all twelve months of the year with those small bones, feet, and butt, a narrow chest and compact body, all set off by a tail that curved in a six inch arc from its base before falling in a shimmering alabaster-white line to the ground.

Spud came to me from Albuquerque via the same home where I bought Ty, but Spud was a gift. My place must have had an invisible Statue of Liberty pleading, "Bring me your tired, your poor, your hungry," because I had two rescue dogs, one abused horse, and a one-eyed stallion, so why not a homeless three-year-old green-broke Arab?

Some horses had personality—they were born with it, people nurtured it, and soon, it was visible to all. The little gray Arab would stand at my shoulder and patiently wait for me to grab a flake of alfalfa or some grain. If I walked away to do something else, he followed a distance behind. Nine times out of ten, I gave in, and a small flake of alfalfa landed on the ground. After a few minutes, his high tail waved goodbye to me as he ran to join the other horses who had long since given up hope of more feed. He was like an annoying three-year-old kid; I didn't put up much of a fight though.

An extra blanket pad helped my saddle fit snugly on his narrow withers. On our first ride, he never bucked; he just ran like a bat out of hell around the corral. Then he stopped in a millisecond, stood still, turned his head, and looked back at me—left side, then right side—and sighed as if to say, "She's still there." We rode over rangeland, and he became accustomed to the rocks, uneven land, gates, barbed wire fences, cattle, javelinas, coyotes, mule- and white-tail deer. He filled out like Ty with long lean muscles, and the memories of the life of leisure on irrigated farm land in New Mexico faded with each day.

His first sight of a cow caused the Arab spin. At least, that was what I called it: one hind foot placed solidly on the ground as the entire body swirled around that foot in a 360 degree turn, a reiner's dream spin. He did not go forward, only snorted and backed up.

"That, my dear friend, is a cow. You will learn to love them and hate them. They are unpredictable in some ways, predictable in others. Get used to them. We share this land with 400 of their kind," I told him as we walked forward to a windmill and a round metal water trough where cows and calves enjoyed their morning drink. We advanced slowly and spun back rapidly... many times. Patience became my best friend. A half-hour or so later, the cows and Spud drank side by side at the drinker.

It's tough to handle change or different ways of doing things for anyone, I guess, but on a ranch, ideas are pretty much set in stone unless proven otherwise multiple times, and even then, people have to think about them some more. With that in mind, I might as well have been riding a gazelle for the amount of enthusiasm the cowboys displayed when I trotted to the upper corrals to help gather an outlying pasture. I read their minds: "She'll be useless on this gather." It didn't help that the high strung three year old had no experience with cattle, but he'd learn, I hoped. Training took time and the more under-the-brim-of-cowboy-hat smiles I caught, the more determined I became to make him a cow horse.

Spud burned up energy as we moved the cattle from the far corners of the pastures, and he learned that it wasn't entirely necessary to rev up that four barrel engine at all times. We rode drag, moving the slow cows and baby calves in the back of the herd to the corrals. One mile became three miles of turns to the right, to the left, back and forth. He about trampled a few calves at first but eventually settled down.

"Ah-h-h-h, we made it in one piece, Spud," came out of my mouth as the corral gate closed, and no major catastrophes were left behind.

We left the cows and calves after they mothered up and grazed in their new pasture. Bob and Ruben loaded their horses on the trailer and headed back to the headquarters. Spud and I jogged the mile and a half home. Head low, steady pace, focused on the dirt trail ahead, the small horse was worn out.

The first six months on the ranch, he must have seen UFOs flying overhead or heard something a hundred miles away that caused his brain to flash DANGER, resulting in unexplained spooks. Constant riding and working mellowed him out some but never squeezed dry that red alert feeling. I learned to appreciate this quirk and realized he did see something and most likely, we'd come up on it or it would pass by us. Sometimes a deer ran through the manzanita bushes, or we passed a dead fire left by illegals or saw a lone bull under a tree, and other times—who knows?

A fence surrounded the house's yard, kept cattle and horses out, and allowed flower beds to flourish in peace. However, the four apple trees in the front yard close to that fence lured Spud, who in turn led the other horses for closer inspection of the trees' fruit. From the time Spud showed up on that land, the pantry stored fewer applesauce jars for the winter.

The gate didn't fare much better than the apples. His hind hoofs kicked the boards and eventually, the hook popped out of the metal circle and the gate swung open. A heavy iron link chain stopped that trick. His four feet stopped at the sound of crinkling paper, his head turned and rested on my extended foot in anticipation of my snack bar's sweet grain. Athena played hide and seek with him in the pasture as Spud chased the dog into the yard, but just slow enough to let her win. She'd run back out chasing him but never fast enough to get hit by a hind hoof.

His shoulders and chest continued to muscle up and fill out as time and miles clicked by; the once-strange environment became mundane and life settled into its rhythm. His education became evident. Barbed wire scars on his chest showed me he learned not to rub or push against the six strand wire fences. Better to shade up under the big oak tree in the pasture's corner during summer's midday heat and save the energy because the job consisted of long days. Oh, and as soon as that cow turned back to the herd, stop and turn also. No need to waste steps.

I bought a bright red wool Mexican saddle pad with leather on the edges, and it contrasted nicely against his light gray coat. The leather tooled bridle with black and white horsehair tassels hung on either side of his cheeks; it helped keep flies away and complemented his Arab head. We covered miles on a nice slow easy jog, while the unadulterated sun added more spots to my arms, a few more wrinkles on my face, and thinned the skin on my hands just another micrometer. I really didn't care. Life was good with ol' Spud, who learned quickly, ate my apples, got his extra hay, and never paid any attention to, "There goes Lisa on that goddamn A-rab," said by some, I imagine, when they spotted the pale horse and his rider on the horizon.

Spud and I, family album

Drenched

Instinctively I jumped and caught my breath as the wind slammed a door shut. Another flash lit up the world, and lightning bolts sped across the sky in pursuit of a place to make their marks.

A gray curtain of rain started the move across the Valley and obscured rangeland—the outside world ceased to exist. The afternoon's performance of A Summer Rain began.

Thunder drum rolls and cymbals clashed in the skies signaling lightning's cue to strike. A flash hit the ground just north of the house. A few years before, a bolt struck the headquarters' living room chimney; bricks flew, bounced off the roof, and landed in the yard.

The wind picked up the beat and pushed tall grass level with the ground. Tree limbs became hip-hop dancers gyrating to the storm's tempo. Leaves were ripped from their homes and never returned. Years ago, my horse Michael lay in the pasture like a broken marionette with his brown hide scorched and naked after one of these storms.

Random white lines struck their targets indiscriminately and without conscience.

Incessant rain pellets bounced off the dirt's trampoline-like floor. The ground didn't get a chance to absorb moisture on its first landing, so drops bounced back up in air, split into thousands of tiny molecules, dropped again, and destroyed the ground's resistance. Within minutes, water ran off steps and roofs as dirt absorbed what it could, and the remaining moisture took a scattershot approach covering the land.

Thirty minutes passed. From the dining room window, I saw the solid curtain of rain transformed into a piece of loosely woven lace; an outline of trees appeared along the Santa Cruz River. The hills of Mexico held either end of a rainbow, and I thought maybe Pancho Villa really did bury treasure there, as the old timers said. Sounds of water looking for resting places filled the air. Rivulets pushed their way to the ground from trees and roof tops. The unmistakable perfume of a summer rainstorm permeated the house when I opened windows. The cool air smothered July's pent-up heat quickly.

With that kind of rain, the Santa Cruz was going to run. I drove to the river and left soft deep canyons on clay roads while chunks of red mud glommed on the truck's sides. Rushing water through the pasture ironed the grass flat, forming small lakes perfect for water bugs and toads.

I rode in the back of the pickup as a kid so many times to watch the river run. Wet dirt splattered all over my arms and Levi's as Mom drove down to the bridge west of the farm, and we'd wait for the trickle of water to appear at the river's bend. The river bed under the bridge wasn't more than thirty-feet wide, bank to bank, and most days three big steps would take you across the water. Stream was a more accurate word. Some months, the bed was dry.

I walked onto the bridge and looked north. Small veins on the land filled with water, ran over the Valley's terrain, followed the downward slopes, fed into the river's main artery, and continued on to Mexico.

The first few trickles went by me like baby's fingers as they crawled along a floor. Within minutes, the river became a frothing mass filled with limbs, fence posts, wire, and muck. Bank to bank, the water swept all in its path to an unknown destination. The storm's aftermath rolled along as the river surged and swelled below me. Wire-wrapped boulders attached to overhanging fence wire were left on the ground to help the fence withstand the water's strength. Break-away water gaps split apart as the water rushed through. Sometimes the water won, crashing against the fence, moving the boulder, and sweeping away entire sections of fence and anything else in its path.

The sound of the running river silenced all other noise; the smell of moisture along with the cooler temperature mesmerized me, lost in flowing water. I saw a cow on top of a hill, and my trancelike state broke instantly. I visualized cattle walking through broken fences and wandering through the busted wire into Mexico.

The next day I rode to the river. When I saw the ranch truck in the distance, I was glad I never had to fix the water gaps after one of these storms. I'd seen the scenario for so many summers at the headquarters. The men threw a couple of rolls of barbed wire, some steel fence posts, shovels, and long steel bars in the ranch truck's bed and left for the day long job.

They waded in knee-high rubber boots through mud and silt and replaced broken fence posts, their gloved hands repositioning barbed wire. As they drove on to the next pasture, the truck's rear view mirror reflected broken fences upright again and wires taut against each post. Wire-wrapped boulders secured the fence line once again. By day's end, mud covered Levi's and work shirts filled plastic laundry baskets, empty rubber boots stood outside the back door, and sweat stained hats hung on hat racks.

I sat on my horse and looked at the river bed which was again a small stream in places, pools of water in others. Yellow butterflies played in the willows, frogs jumped into newly formed puddles, and clumps of river grass looked like they had met a steam roller. Newly exposed brown and red river walls baked in the sun as a gopher frantically scampered over unfamiliar ground and looked for his old home.

Santa Cruz River after a summer rain

Land's Cradle

The windchill factor rose up a notch as ashen clouds drifted across the afternoon sun. The long johns under my Levi's, the silk wild rag tied around my neck, the flannel-lined Levi jacket—they couldn't compete with the bitter blasts that galloped through the Valley. I rode Ty, his chocolate coat in full winter growth, through Pasture 17 on the ranch's north end. With his head tucked down to avoid the wind, he jogged along the cow trail while his tail blew in a forty-five degree angle, ebony hairs hit the saddle's stirrup. The dark bay Arab avoided gopher holes and rocks, followed the dirt trail as it wound over the soft rolling range, and broke into a quick trot as my spurs urged him on to outpace the oncoming rain.

From a distance, the Black Angus/Hereford cattle looked like spots of soot on an oat-colored canvas. Most of the herd had already left the flatland for protection in the hills, but a few stragglers had waited and could be seen along the slopes. The Huachuca Mountains and their indigo ridge lines looked ominous as the cloud cover made its way across the Valley's floor.

Ty, sure-footed and confident in the ground beneath him, trotted up hills, along the ridges, dropped down into small valleys, and loped across the easy stretches of land. My eyes constantly looked for the lone cow, a sure sign of a mother-to-be. She'd wander off from the herd and calve in the privacy of a canyon wall, a hill's incline, or tall winter grass.

The cows in this pasture had carried their babies for three seasons. The animals withstood summer's heat and the monsoon rains that pelted water drops on their hides, while the blue grama grass welcomed the moisture and gained more height during the summer's growing season.

As the leaves turned a stoneground mustard color, the monsoon pillow clouds floated away, and cattle grazed on dried shafts of side oats and black grama grass. Sacaton bushes lost their feathery tops, and their big bunchy clumps looked like old broom heads turned upside down. Squirrels stocked their pantries with acorn nuts, which carpeted the dirt under the live oak trees. Coyotes, javalinas, muledeer and pronghorn antelope, cows, and horses shared the dwindling summer rain water in the dirt tanks with migrating blue herons on their way south to Mexico.

When Christmas time arrived, the cows' bellies looked like barrels of oil between four legs. I felt just plain sorry for the range cows. They carried sixty to seventy pounds of extra weight, maneuvered up and down rocky hills, and trundled along the flatlands.

Two hundred and sixty-five days, give or take a few, had gone by for the pregnant cows, and since mid-January, we had been checking the cattle a couple of times a week to make sure there weren't any calving problems. This day wasn't any different—cows grazed, weather did what it wanted, chickens got fed, and I rode.

Ty's ears flicked forward, and we both spotted a big black buoy in the sea of old bunch grass with two tall Sacaton grass clumps in back of her. Above, the clouds looked heavy and wet. Could she have picked a worse time to calve? Between the wind and the rain, the ground would be so cold and so wet; how do these animals make it, I thought, as I pulled the cuffs of my jacket over the tops of my gloves. The survival instinct and inherent strength of these range animals—truly amazing. We stopped and waited for movement.

The cow's head pointed up the hill, but when she saw us, she lifted herself on her side, then onto her belly and extended her front legs to get up. We backed up, I didn't want to frighten her more and break the labor's cycle. She fell back down on her side, and the wind's current carried the groan to my ears. Her head and neck extended with the tension of a contraction, and she pushed out the sac. Another moan, that deep bellied, heavy cry reverberated from the stomach and out through the throat—like something gut-punched you from the inside—THAT PAIN echoed in the air. I winced at the sound and remembered those labor pains, the hours before my sons were born— wanting it all over. I felt for this old range cow, going through the agony alone, slanted on a hill. Dirt entered her mouth with each breath, and not a speck of sun poked through the menacing clouds to warm her exposed body.

My mind saw the scene that distance blocked. With that final push, a slick head with its bare pink lips, which covered small teeth, pushed through the sticky thick filament which held the newborn for eight and one-half months. The calf's wet silky black body followed, slithering out and down on the hardened pebble encrusted dirt. His tiny white hooves scraped the ground as nerve cells responded to air as it entered his system. The experienced cow hoisted her body with the determination of a climber ten feet from the summit. Her stocky front legs and split hoofs gave a push as she stood up, staggered momentarily, and regained balance. The black tail held trails of the bloody membrane gathering dust as she moved to clean her calf. Like a wide, dull pink spatula, her tongue lapped the milky film off the calf's face while the small head twitched like a horse's head shaking off a pesky fly.

The tongue, as wide as my hand, licked her baby's smell into her sensory system. The small shiny white head and black body couldn't escape the constant bathing action. The movement reminded me of cleaning a saddle—slow deliberate circular motions of removing the grime until the natural sheen came through. This cow would be able to find her calf among a thousand others simply by this one act of tasting and inhaling the calf's unique smell. A time immemorial action, a two-minute bleep on life's screen, bonded these two creatures again.

We walked a little closer, and the calf's head lifted up. I sat there silently, respected another one of nature's miracles, and felt privileged to watch new life come to existence on the land's bassinet.

We moved on, quietly making a wide arc around the pair. I thought about that cow with her newborn. In a few days, she'd leave her baby curled up, belly filled with milk and asleep, hidden in the sacaton clumps while she walked to water and eased her screaming dry throat. Like a carrier pigeon's homing instinct, she'd find her hidden baby again. Within the week, the newborn would have the strength to follow her, and the pair would slowly walk down the trails and join the herd.

Made me think of my own two sons, and I wondered where they were, probably still at work or getting ready to go home. Images flashed in my mind of the kids as they followed me when we boarded airplanes and returned to the ranch for Christmas time or other vacations. Forgotten pictures became movie screens in the mind, and sacred memories titled the marquee.

As quick as that reel started to roll, the wet drops pushed the stop button. I leaned forward, Ty broke into a lope, and we headed home, splattering mud behind us. The rain did a steady flow off the barn's tin roof while I brushed Ty's coat and wished the old cow and calf could be protected under the barn's roof, too. But they would still be outside in the cold.

Years ago, on a day like this one, I got off the school bus and found three newborn lambs by the kitchen's wood stove. Their mothers died giving birth, and one of the cowboys picked up the fuzzy animals, their spindly legs hanging down like new sprouts from a vine, and placed them on a blanket by the wood stove. Three lambs on gunnysacks by the kitchen's wood stove looked like a living nativity tableaux.

Eventually the deluge stopped; Ty trotted out to find his friends. I walked up the muddy hill to the house on a wet and windy February afternoon.

Sharp Springs

Fall

Smoke rose in chimneys; pumpkins and acorn squash sat in kitchen bowls; autumn soup recipes littered kitchen tables; the sun stayed in bed a little longer and cued foliage that its time on the planet was short. A kaleidoscope of orange, yellow, and mocha tints dotted cottonwood leaves, and upon catching a fall breeze, they drifted casually to the ground.

Morning moisture sat on the tiring foliage, while plants' roots sucked liquid for winter storage. Grasses' discarded their green uniforms for drab russet pants and swayed arthritically with fall's breath.

Coolin' off but it'll warm up by 10 or so.
Chainsaw ripping through limbs for firewood.
Weaning calves.
Alfalfa and barley fields, stubble now.
Flannel shirts and wild rags.

Dried grass, birds heading south.
Clouds traveling overhead, too busy to stop.
Dry roads, dirt tanks holding summer rains.
Selling calves and paying down the bank loan.

The Mexicans referred to the town of Lochiel as *La Noria* (the well), its original name since the late 1800s. The once populated town has cottonwood trees that line a little creek and is nestled into low hills within a mile of the Mexican border.

After Colin Cameron arrived in the mid-1800s and settled at the ranch, he named the town Lochiel, because the area reminded him of his Scottish roots. The mist in the Valley rests on the tops of the cottonwood trees that follow the river, invades their limbs, and overshadows the ground below. Never is it so vivid than when the season flips its page to fall.

The air that day was moist and crisp, and I imagined Cameron closed his eyes and saw the moors of his homeland. But I rode my horse and kept my eyes open. The animal brushed against grass seed heads. I watched a red ant push a seed toward his home shaped like a volcano and wished I had that determination at times. The horse and I continued on, making our way down the beige hills and onto the flatlands which were a mass of dry summer forage that would hold the cattle through the winter, I hoped.

A view from the porch, family album

And the Gate Slams

My feet swung out of bed and wiggled their way into slippers on the brick floor. As coffee brewed, I added logs to the two wood stoves, still warm from the previous night's fire, in the kitchen and living room. Predawn's silence and solitude quieted my thoughts, and I savored the early morning coffee. The first sips hit the taste buds and woke up the brain. They trickled down the throat, seeping into my stomach as an Ah-h-h sensation and warmth filled my body.

My favorite time of the day was the morning—the bedcovers hadn't been rolled off the land yet.

Athena stretched on her cushion close to the living room's wood stove and gave me her time-to-go-out look. She slowly walked out to do her morning ministrations. Within minutes, she signaled with the let-me-in door-scratching and returned to her pillow. It was early for both of us, but the semitrucks were to be at the corrals by 8:00 a.m. for the fall shipping.

The elm tree's outline appeared through the big living

room window, which signaled it was time to start the day. Some more coffee, an egg, a piece of toast, and Athena's breakfast, and by 5:15 a.m. we walked down to the barn to feed and saddle Spud.

"Stay, Athena!" I said as Spud and I walked by the house. Reluctantly she lay down, head between her paws, as her black eyes continued to look up at me woefully. Eventually after a series of how-could-you-forget-me barks, she would meander into the yard, curl up under an apple tree, and go to sleep.

Spud and I continued trotting on the two-track road that led to the shipping corrals on the ranch's north end. During the mile and one-half ride, the horizon lit up slowly, and a rough-out of the Huachuca Mountain range became visible in the east. The range's deep blue crests diminished the hills of Mexico to the south but magnified the rolling stretches of grassland surrounding me. Country sounds broke the silence: a bawl, a coyote yelp, and a rhythmic beat on the dirt from horseshoes. The sky displayed shades of gray, off-white, and filmy blues that blended into each hue's edge like a paper sample of pale blue from a paint store. It was going to be a clear day, thank goodness. By the time I reached the corrals, saddled horses stood tied to horse trailers, and it looked like everyone was ready to go to work.

"*Hola, Lisa. ¿Qué pasó?*" (Hello, what's up?)

"*Hola, Ruben.*"

"Hey, Lees."

"Morning, Bob."

"Hey, Larry, Maria, what's up?"

"Not much."

"Damn cold riding down here, I'll tell you that," I said as I pulled the scarf a little tighter on my neck.

Ruben, my brother, cousins, and I rode out to bring in two hundred head of Black Baldies that had spent the night in the shipping pasture. On horseback, we fanned out, slowly moving the cows and calves into the big corrals and then into various small pens. We didn't talk much, just yelled *"vaquilla"* if it was a heifer or *"novillo"* for a steer as Ruben opened and closed gates. Since heifers and steers received different prices, they were weighed separately and put in different pens. A couple of old cows remained and provided some comfort for the soon-to-be-orphans.

Within an hour, the animals were separated. Newly weaned calves stood yelling for their mamas, cows hollered back, and older calves milled around. The horses, grateful to be on the sidelines, stood at the fence rail with saddles loosened some at the cinch. Finally, the sun reached the southern Arizona skies. We leaned on the truck, wiped dust off our faces, and drank some coffee while we waited for the livestock trucks.

Luther, the cattle buyer who'd been buying San Rafael stock for years, and two semitrucks showed up right on time and brought a healthy dose of dust with them. We heard the long haul trucks with empty livestock trailers as they lumbered over cattle guards and dirt roads and traveled through the Valley. By the time the first truck downshifted and clattered over the cattle guard at the top of the hill, our empty coffee cups sat on the tailgate. We were ready to weigh the calves and load 'em up.

Two truck drivers with wrinkled shirts and Levi's

climbed down from the cabs, waved hello, and stretched their bodies. Pulling a baseball cap off his head and running his hand through what was left of his hair, one of them yelled out, "Coffee?" Someone yelled back, "On the blue truck's tailgate."

The night before, we cleaned and balanced the long wood enclosed weighing platform and oiled the gates. Luther and Bob adjusted the livestock scale one more time before the calves entered the enclosure.

Moving calves through the pens wasn't much different than a production line in Detroit. Human links in an interconnected chain kept the calves moving quickly. Gates opened and closed, calves in groups of ten were weighed and put in different pens, while another set of calves took their place on the scales. Throughout all this, mamas and babies bellowed, looked for each other and drowned our attempts at extended conversation.

"So, what do you think this group weighs?" I yelled to Larry, my cousin.

"6,000 pounds. Soggy calves," he yelled back.

"How 'bout this batch?" I yelled as another group scrambled onto the platform, and the gate slammed shut as the metal bar slid into the metal hook. The scared calves jostled against the wood boards, each one trying to find security someplace.

"3,900 pounds. Just weaned, a little light."

"Should weigh more; we had good rains."

Our running commentary didn't stop until the last batch of teenagers ran off the platform and into another pen. The calves peed all over the scales and occasionally shot fountains of manure spraying us and the ground. Calves entered the scales with black hides spotted with green traces of digested grass; our hands ended up with dirt encrusted fingernails and dust and grime covered Levi's and shirts.

A truck driver had backed the trailer to the end of the loading chute, and he stood on the chute's wood platform and waited for us to open the gates. The black and white calves, none older than nine months, scrambled up the chute and followed one another, scared and unsure, frantically looking around for their mamas. Some tried to turn around and blocked the other calves behind them. With cattle prods and sticks, we urged the young animals along the enclosed narrow chute into the truck's ventilated metal compartments.

The Black Angus crossbreds filled the different compartments inside the trailer, and we heard metal doors sliding down the rails and crashing shut. Another section was filled to capacity. Truck drivers in their eighteen-wheelers, now filled with 90,000 pounds of live beef, shifted the engines into low gear and hauled up the hills and out of the Valley on their way to Texas winter wheat fields.

The engine sounds faded with distance, and the cows' plaintive cries for their babies filled the air as Spud and I headed back home after a lunch of chili and tortillas. As the apple trees and the house came into view, Athena bounded down the road to greet us, and we all continued on to the barn. With the horse unsaddled and fed, I settled in on the living room window seat, and Athena jumped up on the other side and laid her head on my outstretched legs. I remembered taking Michael to the airport to fly to Vermont for college. I leaned against the departure area wall and cried that empty feeling out of my gut. It wasn't any different from those two hundred range mothers who looked in the direction of the departed trucks, their mouths open as they called in vain for their babies, but their calves were lost forever. All this was caused by gates slamming and diesel engines roaring—every year the same thing happened.

The next day the cattle still remained along the corral's fence waiting and wailing. By evening time some grazed in the pasture; others kept up their vigilance with parted jaws, heads stuck up in the air and bawled like old, off-key trombones.

A week later, I rode through the pasture and passed contented grazing cows with dried up milk bags and, most-likely, tiny calves in their bellies.

Hereford cow

The Valley's Matriarch

It's been fourteen years now, it's 2013, but it still doesn't seem that so many years have gone by since I left the ranch. The road going west from the headquarters over to the old Heady-Ashburn Ranch, now the San Antonio Ranch, is covered with weeds and grass, and sacaton clumps have claimed more territory. My SUV doesn't have the clearance for that road, so I drive up to the headquarters, now part of the Arizona State Parks system.

Nobody comes out of the house and I won't go up there. I've heard the State Parks staff has fixed up the inside of the house very nicely. I can see from the barn that the outside has been painted, and the windows are painted with contrasting trim. It looks like a movie set to me.

I guess it is better they did change things. It no longer looks like the house I grew up in with my mom, two sisters, and a brother, and all the cowboys that came and went. So, that is another separation, another step. Still won't go inside, nope, I'll keep my memories untarnished.

It has taken me some time to get to this point of

detachment from the San Rafael Ranch, which isn't saying much—on a scale of 1 being none and 10 being lots—I'm at a high 3. I have listened to advice from friends for years now: "Just be in the moment," "Do meditation," "Go on Buddhist retreats," "Travel and get it out of your system," or my favorite, "Just let it go, Lisa." I felt like saying, "Yes, you let your life go right now and let me know what that feels like." I know friends were trying to help, though. I did try all those things, and they helped some, but time has proved to be the healer, that and writing.

I walk through the corrals and follow an old cow trail to where Mom is buried. I like to say "Hi" when I'm down here in the Valley. I will be in Taos for the winter, so it'll be awhile before I get back to Arizona.

A collage of sepia images blends into one another and passes through my mind as the dry air immediately sends me back in time: grandkids playing on the porch and Mom locking the front door to keep the grandkids out "for just a little while, PLEASE!" Janie, my sister, skimming through *The Gold Cookbook* on Thanksgiving Day, and Mary clipping fall foliage to decorate the dining room table. Bob, in a beige long sleeved work shirt, fingers in the pockets of his Levi's, a light gray felt cowboy hat tilted back some on his head, standing with his weight on the heels of his cowboy boots looking at the barn from the front porch. Clear window panes frame these recollections.

It's peaceful this morning; not a breeze, nothing disturbs the sun's rays as I walk slowly on the old cow trail. The grass is dried up, and the scrubby cat's claw bushes have lost their bloom. Now they're just spiny branches waiting to snag a Levi or cause a horse to step aside some. My boot kicks a rock off the path blocking the way for a little black stink bug trundling along. It's so quiet. That's what I miss.

I wonder what happened to the two old glass kerosene lanterns that stood on the kitchen counter ready for use, just in case the Koehler generator didn't turn on at night, which happened more than once in a while. The cowboys laughed as they called those dark nights *una noché romantica* (a romantic night). Now why did that pop into my mind? That thought, along with a vision of grandkids playing in the barn and flying kites on Easter morning and the smell of burning oak in the fireplace and Christmas tamales on the stove.

Maybe some day I'll get the courage to walk into the big house and see the changes. I wonder if the front door was changed? Mom didn't bother to take the imitation stained glass off the front door's window after *The Great White Hope* movie crew left in 1961. The set designers had swabbed a pale wash on the glass leaving a small portion clear. Then they piped in banner format, *The Great Oak*, on the glass, which was the movie's name for the ranch. A minor detail overlooked by them was that the tree in front of the house was a large cottonwood, not an oak tree. The door always provided yet another good "movie story."

The Sears installation men thought they had driven to the end of the earth when they arrived from Tucson to install wood shutters on all the middle floor's windows and carpeting in the bedrooms. When they came out in 1962, it was my first inkling that living on the ranch was different to other people.

"Hey, what do YOU DO out here, young lady?"

"I ride, help the cowboys, drive the tractor, help Mom with the books. I don't know," a typical twelve-year old's answer I thought at the time.

"How about TV?"

"I go over to John and May Gates, our neighbors, to watch *Bonanza*. They have TV."

"Oh. Don't you get bored or lonely?"

I didn't say "How can I get bored when I have my horse and ride with the cowboys?" Instead I just said, "No," and walked on down to the barn. At age eighteen, I couldn't wait to leave, but at twelve, it was equivalent to nirvana for a girl with her own horse.

No matter what the size of the Christmas tree, it was never dwarfed in the living room. One year, Mom bought a big brown and black stuffed gorilla and put it under the tree for Charlie. He walked down the hall into the large room, saw the gorilla, which was about the same size as his four-year-old frame, and screamed bloody murder. He would only return with his personal bodyguards on all sides: Mom on the right, me on the left, and Michael, his older brother, in front.

Christmas was a time of tamales filled with red chili and ranch beef. During the 1960s May Gates brought her famous giant cinnamon roll muffins for Christmas morning breakfast. In 1963 we spent our first Christmas at the ranch, decorated the tree with pine cones, Mexican tin ornaments, and strung cranberries since our ornaments were still in California.

An archway from the living room led to the hall, which

was lined with four bedrooms with three bathrooms and the small kitchen. After living there for a few years, Mom added a small TV room, big enough for three or four people. We only received two channels, high antennas and all. Books on world history, music composition, farm production, Thomas Merton essays, and Agatha Christie novels filled the bookcases, which lined the halls. Rachel Carson's 1963 landmark book, *Silent Spring* lay on one table. I wonder what happened to the green leather books with the titles *Better Soil: Higher Yield* or *Soil Fertility and Animal Health* by William Albrecht, Ph.D. Those two books played a pivotal role in Mom's management of the ranch.

Dr. William Albrecht lectured coast to coast on agricultural ecology before the word environmentalist became a label. He believed the soil needed to be fed, and animal health stemmed from soil nutrients which, in turn, fed the crops. Albrecht developed the base level requirements that are used to this day.

His books were Mom's farm bibles for years when planning the needed soil nutrients for the farm. After she got the soil analyzed, conversations and letters went back and forth between Dr. Albrecht and herself about the proper percentages of minerals needed for a particular crop and for the soil. Once a year, all the corral manure was hauled on the trailer to the farm and spread on some of the fields. Concrete irrigation ditches ran with calcium and magnesium and other nutrients. She walked over the fields and examined the crops and invasive weeds. She understood more and more as each season changed and years went by.

For decades even before Mom arrived, the farm produced an average of two hundred tons of hay a year. Bales of oats, barley, and alfalfa filled the barns and red clover and winter wheat covered the permanent pastures.

The environmental movement had taken hold in the 1980s. Radical environmentalists cut fences while university-associated biologists did studies on the fish species that swam in Sheehy Springs and Sharp Springs, and others studied the flora and fauna and bugs and frogs that lived on the ranch. What was common for us intrigued others. We waited while desert tortoises crept along the road during the summer and heard friends say, "Oh look, there's a turtle." We'd just say, "Yup," and keep on driving or riding.

After the publication of *Silent Spring*, we sprayed our vegetable gardens with water and kitchen soap and once with a mixture of chile powder. The last one didn't work: it killed the seedlings. One of the cowboys kept dead grasshoppers and stink bugs in Ball glass canning jars and claimed the smell drove the grasshoppers away. We tried it all except, of course, insecticide.

We never did spray for grasshoppers nor were any non-native grasses ever introduced on the land grant. We ate butter, not margarine because of its additives, and swallowed Bayer aspirin because it was "purer" than Tylenol. No poison-filled baits were used for the coyotes because the vultures would spread the poison in their feces. A spray was used for the cockleburrs, but we were told to wear gloves, don't spray before a rain, and pull out the dead plants and burn them.

On one of the train trips to Arizona, Mom brought

a bucket of dirt with us along with our luggage. As the cab pulled up to the train station, the porter opened the car door and said, "Hello, Mrs. Sharp, off to Arizona this evening?"

"Yes, we are."

As we got out of the back seat, Mom lifted the bucket from the car's floor, put it on the cart, and asked him, "Could you please take this also? Along with our suitcases? Thanks."

He followed us to the ticket office and on to the waiting train. As we walked, he asked, "Uh, ma'am, why are you taking a bucket of dirt with you?"

"It's not just dirt. There are worms in there for the compost pile."

"Worms? Ma'am, you are carrying worms on the train?"

"Yes, now can you please just put the bucket on the bathroom floor in our compartment? The bucket is covered, they won't get out. Thanks," she said as if she was talking about a bag of cookies.

With a look of disbelief, he did as asked, turned to me and said, "I thought worms were for fishing."

"I don't know. All I know is my uncle has worms under his apple trees in Pasadena, and Mom wants some in the compost pile in Arizona, so she brought a bucket of worms with us."

I sat down and began to read *The Black Stallion* while I waited for the train to leave.

Thinking back, I never thought anything odd about living in a house with two kitchens. Both kitchens were equipped with stoves and refrigerators, sinks and counters, but the little one was more convenient for Mom, since it was next to her bathroom and bedroom. She spent most of the time at the ranch house alone while we were in school and my brother was in the Army, and then he subsequently lived with his family at the north end.

Paperwork moved from the little kitchen table to the dining table in the big kitchen, and we did spend some time looking in both kitchens for a single sheet of paper. The office, for Mom, was whichever table she was using at the time. And eventually the papers all ended up in filing cabinets or binders.

After Colonel Greene bought the ranch in 1903, cowboys moved into the house, and lots of changes occurred over the next fifty-five years. Mom said that at one time the entire house had redwood wainscoting. In the early years the south side of the house may have been used for the cowboys with the rest of the middle floor occupied by the ranch manager and his family. That's a possible reason for two kitchens. But as I said, it was my norm as a child, so it never crossed my mind that it was different.

Through all the various holidays while I was in high school, the six fireplaces warmed the rooms throughout the main floor. I'd stand in front of the hall's in-floor central heating grate in a Lanz flannel nightgown ballooning around my legs capturing the rising heat and listen to my sisters and brother tell about their lives outside the ranch. By January first, Mom and I would close the transom windows above two of the bedroom doors and block the heat from going into unoccupied rooms. The next day, we would return to our world of cowboys, cattle, and horses.

As I walk through the pasture now, I look south and see a new windmill breaking the horizon line. Maybe that land has been split up and someone built a house over there. This is why it is hard to come back; seedlings of civilization have begun to sprout.

We used to sit on the front porch during the summer and watch the lightning storms in Mexico beyond that new windmill. It was like watching a light show at a rock concert. For years the lightning was the only light we ever saw in the distance until the late 1960s when Santa Cruz, a small town seven miles south of the border, got electricity. One of the first things Mom did, though, was to repair that porch. Carpenters removed rotting boards and painted lumber with gray paint which contrasted with the light blue ceiling over the porch.

"Well, it's like the sky, Lees," she told me when I asked about the blue ceiling.

The birth of Michael, Mom's first grandchild, made us put up cross rails under the hand railings surrounding the porch. Molly, Mom's English bulldog, poked her head through the wood two-by-fours and barked at visitors. Michael sometimes napped in a crib with Molly snoring underneath the mattress on the enclosed screen porch outside the two bedrooms on the south side. If Michael started to cry, the dog stood and barked at the screen door until we came to pick him up. Thinking back, the cross rails were put up when Molly was a puppy so *she* wouldn't fall off the porch.

I wonder how many hundreds of people walked on the trail, wide enough for one person's boots, that led from the house to the barn. From the porch, it looked like another cow trail. One of the old timers told me lightning struck the ground in the middle of the yard right next to a cowboy who was walking up to the house, and he lived to talk about it. I didn't believe him. But I didn't want to test that statement out either, so it could've happened.

I'd forgotten about all these gopher holes in this pasture. Little mounds of dirt here and there make this area look like one of those space maps of Mars. I stand and wait for a tarantula to pass by and remember Pancho saying to me that when they came out, it signaled the summer rains were ending.

Down the hill, past a couple of oak trees, the wrought iron fence around the gravesite becomes visible. Everything is as it should be: leaves on the ground, lots of grass, dried morning glories on the iron fence. Fall is here.

Every time I come here, I think of Mom and her piano. Sometimes she walked into the office, sat at her piano, and played Bach. Now it seems like such a contrast. But as a child, it was, "Oh, Mom's just playing the piano."

The office was home to the grand piano, an upright piano, and two big wood desks that were rarely used while she lived there. A Steelcase™ filing cabinet stood next to the door and was the only reference to the room's name, The Office. Mom's fingers didn't keep up with time's steady beat, and by the time grandkids filled the house, she only played the scales. Notes drifted out the door and invited the question: And what prompts you to play today? But I never asked her and doubt if anybody else did either.

Why didn't I ask her these questions when she was alive?

I moved into my room the summer of 1963 when I started high school. The small love seat tucked under the room's bay window held dusty Levi's after a day's horseback ride or supported my knee as I peered out to see if the yellow school bus was coming down the road at 7:00 a.m.

Our rooms evolved into a guest room or grandchild's room as our family grew. Michael proudly displayed ownership of his room, next to Grandma's, by writing his name with permanent marker on the wall and small couch. The only room that remained the same until she left the ranch was my mother's. A rosary and a well-worn copy of the New Testament lay on her bedside table. School pictures of her grandchildren sat on the fireplace mantle.

The basement was home to a cowboy or two or three with a wood cook stove and refrigerator, kitchen table, and two single beds. In addition to the "cowboys' room," there was a guest bedroom, my brother's room before he got married, and the meat room where ranch beef hung then was cut, wrapped, and frozen. Three rooms were used for storage of ranch supplies, furniture, and miscellaneous boxes. A painting of a cowboy roping a cow on one of the bedroom walls showed off a hidden talent of some cowboy in the early days. An old water well no longer in use, covered with a big concrete top, caused people to trip if the lights weren't turned on while they rounded the corner to walk up the steps to the main floor. In the big kitchen, we heard the cowboys as they spoke in the kitchen below; on both floors, the morning coffee smells mingled with morning chatter.

Cowboy drawing, family album

Nothing much was ever done to the rooms and bathroom on the top floor—one room had been used as a repair shop, but the others had been bedrooms. Cameron had built a self-contained house to survive Indian attacks and whatever other fears he held and to provide comfort for visitors who stayed for weeks at a time in the late 1890s.

The house moved into the twentieth century slowly. Over time, a washing machine whirled, an electric percolator brewed the morning coffee and eventually, an oxygen tank stood in Mom's bedroom to help with her night breathing. An underground phone line came into the Valley during the late 1960s, and the cable stretched to the big house and accommodated one phone in the hall. We never did get an electric line; generators and solar panels worked fine for us.

With the house perched on a hill, the horizon presented a panoramic view of the mountains of Sonora, Mexico, rolled east to the Huachuca Mountains, and in turn, found north, where the peak of Mt. Wrightson broke the horizon ending up at the Nogales Mountains with the sun saying goodbye before sinking into the evening sky. A person could sit in a rocking chair on the porch, with legs resting on the railings and easily picture days gone by. The only differences between 1898 and 1998 were no light reflections from Nogales and Santa Cruz, no pickups parked at the barn, and no tire tracks on the road. Other than that, we still had the silence broken only by "ribb-it, ribb-it" spoken by frogs in the pond by the house, the jangle of spurs as cowboys walked up to the big house, and the creak of a windmill fan as it completed a cycle. We still had the Spanish words *Hasta mañana* (until tomorrow) spoken as cowboys left for the day.

The day is moving along here; it's about time to walk back to my car. Brushing the leaves off the gravestone, I close the gate so cows can't tromp around inside. The cowboys built a small rock wall around the site like the wall in front of the big house, which Mom had built in the 1970s. That's good, I think, she still has a part of that house here.

It's been a good day, and I'm glad Mom is in this little hidden valley where the view probably hasn't changed much since the Valley was born.

Morning Music

Fireplace size dry oak and piñon wood thumped down into a wood box and their echoes filtered through the house. Water splashed as it filled the milk bucket and signaled the gallon glass jars were full. The porch's screen door closed with a light bang. Recognizable footsteps walked on the porch and down the concrete steps. The morning chores had begun. These four sounds were a constant thread in the early mornings in the big house.

During the summer months, the wood box was empty, but the basement's screen door still banged, and fading conversations followed, as cowboys walked to the barn.

A truck rattled over the cattle guard, parked by the barn, and when the door slammed, the sound carried up to the house. We looked out the window and said, "Who just pulled up?"

The family dog nosed the screen door open, it closed

with a soft tap, and the family pet began her day. Birds sang, horses whinnied, cottonwood leaves rustled; the ranch's daily orchestra surrounded the headquarters and needed no conductor.

An Empty Swing

I can still see this Mexican woman with smiling brown eyes standing in her kitchen, salt-and-pepper hair pulled back into a tight gray bun, a blue and white pull-over-the-head apron with front pockets covering a cotton skirt and blouse, a small gold wedding band worn thin from more than fifty years of marriage on her finger. Gold, flat hoop earrings hang through long-ago stretched holes in ear lobes. She pats and spreads the flour dough as it sails from one hand to the other. With each touch, the disk becomes larger and larger as the round, translucent umbrella lands on her fingers. Sixteen-inch thin, round tortillas, which soak in a singular taste that comes from a cast-iron pan, sizzle on the stove. When done, the cooked beige dough has crisp, mottled brown spots where flecks of lard used to be. White flour, lard, and salt, everything we're not supposed to eat today, cooked and dipped in fresh red chili sauce covering cubed ranch beef—those tortillas were the best I've ever had.

She tried to teach me and slowly spoke in Spanish:

"Make little balls, flatten them and pull the edges out some; start flipping them back and forth between your palms until they expand and expand and expand." The results were thick, uneven, and lumpy cooked discs. "Ay Lisa, you have to practice," she said in Spanish, not a speck of compassion evident for my inability to synch the hand movements to achieve the edible circle. Before round ups, I drove to Lochiel and pulled up in front of Arturo and Lola's house, a Quonset hut from World War II, and the smell of fresh chili greeted me.

"*Hola, Señora,*" I said through the screen door.

"*Pasa, pasa, Lisa* (Come in, come in)."

"*Ay, Lisa ...,*" and she spoke quicker than I understood at times, handed me a fresh tortilla lathered with frijoles, and continued to chatter away. We loaded the truck with a big pot of ranch beef, ground and cubed, which was covered with homemade red chili sauce. A stack of tortillas of various sizes were folded inside a white floursack kitchen towel with the top corner displaying a hand embroidered blue bird or flower. Frijoles or frijoles entero (mashed or cooked pinto beans) finished the menu.

As I walked to the truck, she rattled instructions to me about when I was to get her pots back to her.

"*No llegues tarde, Lisa, y no te olvides nada. ¿Me entiendes?* (Don't be late, Lisa, and don't forget anything. Do you understand me?)

"*Si, Señora,*" I said dutifully.

When the last calf of the day was branded, we placed the food close to the fire and enjoyed the hot chili. The spiciness stayed in our throats long after we closed the corral gates for the day. Definitely, the best part of round up was Lola's food.

When The Nature Conservancy bought the ranch in December 1998, they agreed I could stay on for a few more months. Lola's husband, Arturo, who farmed at our ranch for years, preceded her in death. I don't remember where I was when Arturo died, so I was glad I was here to attend her funeral that spring day.

The small tan church in Lochiel looked lonely perched on top of the hill. Just inside the wood door, I noticed the statues of different saints that Mom bought were still on the wood stands along the walls. When we first moved to the Valley, she asked the priest in Patagonia to come out on Sundays to say Mass. Initially he came weekly, and then once a month until he was transferred to another country parish.

In 1972, I stood in this church where Lola's coffin lies. With my ash blond hair pulled back by a white fabric bow and my grandmother's ivory mantilla draped around my shoulders, I walked down the aisle on my father's arm and stood next to my husband-to-be, a man six years my senior and as many inches taller. At age twenty-two, I said, "I do." We walked past bouquets of dried grasses picked from the ranch's pastures interspersed with bouquets of fresh yellow and white daisies and continued down the aisle to the double wood doors. Tall kerosene heaters took some chill from the chapel, but the guests on the pews still kept their jackets on and scarves tied around their necks.

All my photos were thrown out accidentally during one of my innumerable moves, but I remembered so clearly one photo that was taken from a distance on that January day. The church had a background of thin ivory cirrus clouds under a pale winter sky. College friends with long hair and skirts, flowered blouses and panchos, cowboys with their best felt Stetson hats, and family members congregated by the church's front door. Small groups stood with their heads bent close to one another—a timeless image that inspired a sense of a friendly gathering in the country.

As I walked past the pews towards Lola's coffin, I saw a few old classmates sitting on the church pews and remembered the school bus ride over dirt roads. That body-jarring trip combined with wind and cold that came in through the windows in the wintertime was hard to forget. When I started Patagonia High School, a friend of Mom's was visiting from California.

"I cannot believe there is a school bus in this area taking kids to the school," she said. "I just drove seventy-five miles from Tucson, and once I left Patagonia, I only saw one house."

"There must be other people out here but where?" Her voice and eyebrows rose simultaneously as she looked at me to seek confirmation there was other life on this patch of the globe.

The bus driver, Gordo, kept the school bus at his home in Washington Camp, a tiny old settlement north of the ghost town of Duquesne. At one time, a bar was there that also sold some basic food items. During the school year, he and his two children started down the windy road around

6:00 a.m. Rolling down the canyon, one lane in some stretches and wide enough for two vehicles in others, the bus went through Lochiel where a majority of the inhabitants had the surname of de la Ossa.

In the early 1900s, the de la Ossa family settled in the border town. The only other surnames I ever heard in the town were those of the U.S. Customs officer's family, who lived by the border fence, and the school teachers who lived by the one room schoolhouse.

After eight or so kids boarded the bus in Lochiel, it continued on to the "T" below the San Rafael Ranch headquarters where the Goodwin kids got on after a ten mile drive from their family's ranch. Other children got on the bus throughout the Valley before we dropped down into a canyon. If the roads were dry, we cut through the old Best place and followed the back road to Harshaw. The Hale girls were the first to get on the bus, and we continued down Harshaw Canyon. The bus rattled along, as old cottonwood and sycamore leaves dusted off the roof. Gordo avoided cattle strolling across the road for their morning drink at the creek. Twenty-seven kids boarded that bus from start to finish. There were probably more in earlier years. At the Rocking Chair Ranch turnoff, the constant bobbing and rattling stopped. The bus picked up speed, and it was smooth sailing on paved roads to Patagonia Union High School, where we arrived at 8:10 a.m.

The bus always made me think of a yellow turtle, its nose poking out of a bloated yellow shell trundling along on its preset course. The vehicle and the driver didn't care about weather. They plodded along, and we'd laugh as the bus do-si-do'ed on muddy wet roads, but none of us ever doubted that Gordo would not get us home. By the time my stop came, the cowboys had started the evening chores. I'd change my clothes and ride my mare on hills for no reason at all except to just ride.

A few days before this funeral, I made the entire sixty-five mile drive for the first time since graduation day in May 1967. I drove past the high school and saw three gleaming big yellow Blue Bird school busses in the parking area. I wondered what was the size of their graduating class. Ours was seventeen students in 1967.

After the funeral service, I said hello to the few people who stood outside the church. It was good to see them after so many years, but other than "How is so and so?" and "Do you have kids?"—general questions—conversations became forced, and I walked down the hill to my truck.

Next to the schoolhouse, on the other side of the road from the church, a couple of frayed ropes hung from a big cottonwood's tree limb where a swing used to carry kids during recess. Michael attended preschool there for two months in October 1974. I took a six week maternity leave from work after Charlie's birth, and the three of us went to stay at the ranch. Just doesn't seem possible that in this little place twenty-five years ago, kids ran on dirt roads to each other's houses, dogs barked, and people waved as cars drove by.

At the border fence, I saw the old piece of tin was still there. After the U.S./Mexico border crossing closed here in the early 1980s, someone cut a hole in the border fence and hung a piece of roofing tin over the hole, but people moved the tin to the side when they walked from the U.S. to Mexico or back. It was like a "water gap" in a gully, which kept the water from busting the fence. If there's enough force to get through, the fence'll get broken and it'll open up one way or another, and something or someone will get through.

People weren't as subtle about the fence one mile east of the border crossing. Locals from both sides of the border put in a wire gate along the fence and drove into the U.S. for shopping or drove to Santa Cruz to see family. Cowboys from Santa Cruz would meet someone at the gate and get a ride from there to do day work on one of the Valley ranches. Over time, the one-half mile two-track road going from the border to the county road became part of the road grader's route when it needed to be smoothed out, especially after summer rains.

Everyone ignored the sign:

THIS IS AN ILLEGAL BORDER CROSSING

I drove through Lochiel the other day, the first time in fourteen years since Lola's funeral in 1999. The one room school house and teacher's house are still standing; a non-profit organization has taken over their maintenance. The LOCHIEL COMMUNITY BULLETIN BOARD, a school shop project for some of the town's kids, still stands. Rusty metal bars hold up a peeling plywood board covered with a narrow roof, much like a roof over a narrow bird house. On the board is stapled a U.S. Forest Service flyer, "Prevent Forest Fires," with chicken wire over the flyer. I remember how proud those two kids were when they unloaded their project off the bus and then saw it standing in place that weekend, black and shiny. Wonder what happened to those boys?

My generation has moved away, and bulldozers have razed a few adobe houses. It's as if pages of an Etch-A-Sketch have been lifted up taking with them the times when the Valley and surrounding areas were filled with cowboys and young families lived on ranches. Gone are the cowboys who worked on the ranch and sent their kids to school in town. Gone are the families of miners and farmers who lived in Lochiel; now, their grandkids go visit the town on a weekend to see where *Poppy y Mamá* used to live. Three houses remain. I did see some smoke coming from a chimney at one house, so perhaps a son or grandson is thinking of moving back home. I hope so.

Moving Sand

Living in Albuquerque during the mid-1970s, I drove to the ranch several times every year. On one of these trips, I went up the canyon into the Valley, and a yellow bumble-bee-like splotch on a picture perfect Western landscape hit my eyes. SPLAT!

"Why do we need a picture of a cow on the side of the road out here?" I asked when I saw the county road supervisor on the Valley road.

"So people know there are cows on the road when they're driving out here," he answered.

"What else is out here, zebras? How could anyone driving these roads not know it is open range?"

The UPS truck lived up to its reputation of "We deliver everywhere," propane and gas trucks delivered fuel to ranches, and the vet came out when called. These were the familiar outside-the-valley vehicles. The ranchers knew the neighbors' vehicles. If an unfamiliar car went by, we would say, "Huh, wonder who that was?" And we all knew cows grazed on this land.

Placed at various turns and intersections on the maze of dirt roads, cow pictographs sprung up like unwanted dandelions. In their early stages of growth, when just a few signs and posts found their way into the earth, the cow's image served as wonderful targets. The cow's belly became the bulls eye and after a few well placed shots, pastureland showed through the sign. Others found their way face down in the dirt next to a set of tire tracks. The signs' constant demise kept the county road workers busy for a few months. Eventually visual acceptance morphed into mental acceptance, and the painted tin became part of the landscape along with the dirt, cottonwood trees, and manzanita bushes.

One small sign, a seemingly insignificant minor addition in the world of road maintenance, marked the beginning of change in our ranching world. The rural isolation, with its miles of dirt roads empty of gas stations, proved to be enough of a physical and psychological barrier to stop some people from venturing off the pavement from the surrounding towns of Patagonia and Sonoita, but others took the plunge and braved the Valley roads. They received the optical notification to be aware of the cattle.

A friend of mine from Oregon told me her dad used to say, "Mr. Damn, Mrs. Damn, and the whole Damn family are on the roads today." The San Rafael Valley residents felt that way at times also, when vehicles ran out of gas or took a turn too fast and slid out or got stuck in the mud after a rain. We'd help pull their automobiles from whatever mess they had gotten themselves into. Their last question invariably would be: "How do I get back to town?"

For some people, the signs didn't work. A Valley resident would find an animal lying on the side of the road, and the ranch owner would have to shoot the cow or bull and put it out of its misery.

In the 1980s, tourists began to frequent the Valley more often as SUVs and 4x4 trucks became popular. That 4x4 painted in big slanted lettering on the side of a Ford truck or a Dodge Ram seemed to imply Nothing Can Stop Us, though summer rainy season would find more than one truck stuck in the mud. The wet red clay loved to squish around the tires, gum up the tread, and suck the wheels into its quagmire so they'd spin and form a slick, gooey, smooth canyon in the road while the vehicle sank deeper and deeper into the mud. We'd pass empty sedans left on the side of the road for a few days until a tow truck came and hauled them away, mud and all.

The metal sign with its lonely cow, though, did not prove adequate enough as the visitors increased. The yellow and black signs procreated and produced directional and informational signs over the next three decades:

SHARP TURNS AHEAD
       UNPAVED ROADS AHEAD
              PRIMITIVE ROADS
                      DANGEROUS FOR BICYCLES

Signs with squiggly lines and others with arrows and a sign with a semi truck in a circle and a line across it—all stood along the roads like sentries at their posts. The year 2000 produced:

TRAVEL CAUTION
ILLEGAL IMMIGRATION MAY BE ENCOUNTERED
IN THIS AREA.

With the increase of drug smuggling and the aftermath of 9/11, the U.S. Border Patrol trucks and agents swarmed the roads. They traversed the Valley in trucks and ATVs on the job's required quest.

Along with the cars, trucks, and ATVs, people came with binoculars, floppy hats, and baggy L.L. Bean pants. Early mornings found them parked on the roads as they marked Baird's Sparrow, Horned Lark, Chihuahuan Raven and others off their bird list. Fathers and sons, dressed in camouflage shirts and pants, revved up their ATVs, zoomed up and over the roads, and left a long cloud of dust in the air.

It is selfish of me to think the Valley would remain isolated and only available to its residents. It is unrealistic of me to think it wouldn't be discovered and put on a map someday. Our old ranch headquarters is now San Rafael State Park, so that doesn't help much as far as the Valley anonymity goes.

As I drive through Patagonia on my way to the Valley, I know very few of the residents who now live in the town. I continue on the country road and crest the hill into the Valley. Little has changed. Sky is still gorgeous, no visible phone or power lines, just barbed-wire fences, cattle, and open prairie spread before me.

I continue the drive to my friend's ranch and pass two cars. The drivers don't wave back. I pass an old neighbor who still lives in the Valley; we wave and back up our vehicles to catch up on the local news. He looks at my small black SUV. By the way, this is the same kind of vehicle I used to scoff at, and now I drive one. As Mom always said, "Be careful what you make fun of." Anyway, he says, "Oh, you're the one driving the black SUV. Couldn't figure out who that was driving on the road the last couple of days." No question, some things have remained the same.

New folks have bought ranches out here, and some ranches have been split up into smaller parcels. Twitter, Facebook, and texting bring birders out to check the latest landing of some rare or migrating bird. Entomologists look for bugs and botanists look for exotic fauna. Black Baldies, Black Angus/Hereford crosses, replace the once sought after purebred Hereford cattle. But the land hasn't fluctuated. It still wraps around your body and holds your eyes with its undisturbed vistas. The setting sun flickers on the evening clouds and makes them wonderful shades of orange that cannot be reproduced by man. The undiluted smells of a winter rain or the humidity before a summer rain can still be brought into your body with one small breath.

I traveled to Jordan in 2011 and took a "Desert Jeep Ride" to see the Bedouin camps and the sandstone formations. A desk clerk at the hotel had a friend, who had a friend, etc. The driver, dressed in a traditional Bedouin robe and head covering, was sixty and looked seventy-five. On either side of his dark brown eyes, the skin hung down like wilted leaves and smile lines formed deep crevices on either side and folded down onto his cheeks. His hands, leathery and calloused, didn't seem to fit into place in the context of a tourist jeep driver; nothing about him fit my preconceived idea of a person in the tourist business.

He maneuvered the vehicle over the sand and up to some sandstone hills. I never did see any roads, just ripples on the earth left by the wind. The tire tracks became invisible as sand fell back into the disturbed ground. We stopped at the base of an outcropping, and he made some desert tea (sixty percent sugar and forty percent tea) over a small fire. He told me, in broken English, that he moved from the desert into a small village a few years before. He could make more money doing tourist business because the Bedouin life had become too hard. He couldn't make a living anymore from the animals, so he literally pulled up stake, moved to a village, sold his animals and with the proceeds, bought a "Lady's Jeep."

"What is a Lady's Jeep?" I asked.

"It has automatic transmission, not manual."

"Oh," was all I said.

He went out to the desert by himself sometimes, lay in

the hot sand to ease his arthritic bones, and remembered when all the Bedouins lived off the land and herded their goats, sheep, and camels. Most of these families had moved into villages, but a few still hung on to the old ways. He spoke of black nights and how the stars lit up the sky and the full moon reflected beams off the beige sand. Only the sounds of milling animals and his own breathing echoed in his ears as he lay quietly under the black wool tent in the desert sands of Jordan.

He had to go deeper into the desert to escape the trucks' road noise as they pulled their tractor trailers behind them and roared down the highways, which cut through the desert. Tourist buses filled the roads and took many of the world's nationalities to see Petra, the Dead Sea, the Red Sea, and twelfth century Crusader castles. The buses stopped at a "Bedouin Camp," where postcards were sold and tea was served. "Look at that, a real Bedouin" was probably said more than once and understood by the men in their black thobes (long dresses). But the two of us, we sat on the sandstone rocks, sipped our tea, each lost in our own thoughts and reminisced of days before the signs.

Winter

The corral fence supported my weight as I watched diamond-like droplets snag the sun's rays and shimmer on the corral fence. The beams slowly came over the Huachucas and caressed my skin; their warmth slipped into my body. A truck loaded with hay bales made its way across the frozen ground, tires broke patches of ice, and the engine sound cut through the early morning's frozen air.

Cattle and horses stood like Hindu icons and Greek statues as they faced west while icy particles melted on their hides.

Trees were barren, protein was gone from the grass, the land was like dough waiting for warm weather's yeast to lift its dense brown crusty mass. But until the days got a little longer and the dirt saved the sun's heat, this land was Closed for Winter. It lay still while its inhabitants continued to burrow and wait for warmth's incentive to open its doors.

Frozen water troughs.
Short days.
Matches handy by wood stoves.
A dead calf half eaten by coyotes and vultures.
Dogs curled up by fireplaces.
Down comforters and flannel sheets.
Bare trees, dormant rose bushes, red berries.
Stews, soups, Christmas tamales.
Fires burned all day long.

Silence is the common thread of all four seasons in the San Rafael Valley. I drive out of the grassland, through the canyon and the quietude slips away. Only a toehold remains as the dirt road meets the pavement, which is black all year long.

Lonely Angel

The streamer of blue, red, and white Tibetan prayer flags I brought back from a trip to Bhutan hangs forlornly from the wrought iron fence that surrounds her grave.

Withered morning glory vines stick to the low, black iron fence, and when the summer rains come, they bloom a glorious blue.

A ten-inch-tall Mexican votive candle with a weather bleached image of the Virgen de Guadalupe leans against the smooth granite boulder that marks the south end of the gravesite.

The rock, big enough to sit on and dangle your feet, holds a simple metal cross. Rain has dribbled off the religious icon and left a thin brown line over the "e" in her first name.

Tall grass, the color of dried oats, grows around the granite slab and stops the dried leaves from moving on with the wind. Each time I visit, I rake leaves and dried prairie grass out of the small graveyard, brush nature's debris off the granite slab, and trace my forefinger on her name just so she knows she isn't forgotten. I know touching the letters is more for me.

Florence Greene Sharp
September 18, 1906 – May 14, 1995

Next to the tombstone, a carved black Mexican stone angel from the ranch house garden provides some company for Mom when cows aren't grazing under the nearby trees.

The infamous Black Angel—you would have thought hell had visited the ranch when Mom opened the truck's tailgate. She found the three-foot angel in Nogales, Mexico, brought it back to the ranch house, and asked the Mexican cowboys to place it on the stone walkway. They told her it was bad luck to have a black angel because she signified the Angel of Death. She'd look at them and nod but the black angel remained. After the summer rains started, the jasmine vines grew and covered the prominent black stone used for the statue's base. Sometimes, in the early morning with a coffee cup in hand, I'd see Mom pull vines off the guardian's face so the embedded mica specks in the granite sparkled back at the sun.

My mother died on Mother's Day—a fitting day for her to leave this world. She never liked it—she saw no point in a day designated for mothers. But I think she didn't want the attention; shyness crept into that side of this ranching woman most people never knew. People only saw the business woman who managed a ranch. They passed her on dirt roads as she drove to the farm or upper corrals or out to a pasture to talk about erosion control with Sidney Hatch or Bob Lennon. They heard about her from the movie crews. I saw a woman who cradled Molly when she died, wiped a tear when a colt got snake-bit, and arranged for full-time care when a cowboy's son became a quadraiplegic.

Footpath trails as visible as the I-10 interstate, which brings me from New Mexico to Arizona, skirt her grave. Now patches of grass break the once smooth clay dirt paths since leather soles no longer give the foliage any competition. In 2009, the ten-foot U.S./Mexico border fence stopped most of the illegal immigrants from passing through this high desert area where stars light up the rangeland and mountains are silhouetted on full moon nights. The travelers used to stop at the grave, say a prayer to help them on their journey, sleep under the oak tree, and continue their sojourn. Just a supposition on my part, though, judging by some old clothing and a few votive candles I'd seen on previous visits. They must have felt a solace with the few religious icons marking her grave under the oak tree. Who knows?

My siblings and I searched for a spot on the ranch and found this small hill close to the headquarters. We wanted a place where she could see the cattle, the blue sky, a cowboy or two, and feel protected from the spring wind and summer sun. The Arizona oak tree with its gray twisted limbs gives a bit of shade over the gravesite and allows a person to sit and talk to her on sunny days.

A jigsaw puzzle of small clouds and blue skies vie for my attention as I remember the days of horseback riding across the ranch to visit the grave. I unloaded my horse from the horse trailer at the ranch's north end and rode six miles on cow trails, up and down grass covered hills under the unfiltered sun to the south end of the ranch. Arthritis prevents me from riding now, so instead, I drive on an abandoned road, park, and walk the remaining distance to say hello.

I sit on the stone steps in front of the plot's iron gate and see the wide expanse full of green grama grass, yellow goldenrod, and gray sage. Green dots of oak and cottonwood trees break up the Valley's sea of grass until the wave hits the base of the cobalt blue, scraggy Huachuca Mountains. An occasional cow's bawl and a bird's song pluck the symphony's strings; their notes drift over me and the dirt, grass, rocks, hills, and arroyos.

We thought about burying her in the small cemetery in the country town of Patagonia, twenty-two miles northwest of the ranch, but she wouldn't have liked that. This is her home, this valley of ranching country. This is where she belongs. If she had been buried in town, she couldn't get away and go back to the ranch. Where would she get her solace then?

We never imagined we wouldn't be here when we buried her on this knoll. We retained some acreage on the ranch's north end with thoughts of possibly returning at some point in our lives. We also retained ownership of this one acre of land where I am sitting at this moment.

It isn't easy to visit her now—distance, old dirt roads, and locked gates. It is hard to ask permission to cross the land—just doesn't seem right since it was our family's ranch for four generations. In the West, ranches have forgotten names on fallen tombstones, which mark the transit of land from familiar hands to new owners. It isn't unusual to see a lonely grave. But this grave is my mom's.

Deep breaths bring the high desert country air into my body, and I smell the summer scents of green grass, earth, and the previous night's rainwater. A few red ants crawl up the toe of my cowboy boot, but they don't find anything worthwhile to take back home, so they make their way back onto the dirt.

In fifty years, I imagine the black stone angel will be eroded and covered with a faded blanket of scraggly old vines. By then, my tombstone will be found in the clay dirt near my mother's, and squirrels will scamper over the granite slabs to hide acorns for the winter months. But for now, I will continue to make the drive from New Mexico to Arizona, will clean the gravesite, and tell Mom about her grandkids and great-grandkids.

I am still.

I quiet my breathing.

I close my eyes.

Every ounce of my soul melts into the surroundings, and I become one with this land that will always be my home.

San Rafael Valley grasslands

There is only this solid sense of having had or having been or having lived something real and good and satisfying, and the knowledge that having had or been or lived these things I can never lose them again. Home is what you can take away with you.

—Wallace Stegner, *Marking the Sparrow's Fall,* 1998.

Appendix

San Rafael Ranch Filmography

I compiled this list from Tucson Film Commission records, historical papers, and memories. Many "shoots" are not included due to the family's request for the ranch's privacy. Because of this, some films are not mentioned, nor are numerous commercials filmed over the years. I apologize to those crew members and cast.

1950s
Oklahoma

1960s
The Great White Hope
Heaven with a Gun
McClintock

Maverick episode
Wild Rovers

1970s

The New Maverick
The Young Pioneers
Tom Horn

1980s

Little House on the Prairie
Blue Moon

1990s

The Fantastiks
Arizona Dream
Pontiac Moon
Young Guns II

Books Referencing San Rafael Cattle Company

Hartman, G. Marshall, Ralph Tanner Associates, *The Making of a Cowman*, 1992.

Sharp, Robert L., University of Arizona Press, *Bob Sharp's Cattle Country*, 1985.

Sharp, Bob, Nighthorses, *Eight Valleys A Linked Landscape*, 2012.

Sonnichsen, Charles L., University of Arizona Press, *Colonel Greene and the Copper Skyrocket*, 1974.

Stewart, Janet Ann, University of Arizona Press, *Arizona Ranch Houses*, 1974.

Lisa Sharp

About the Author

Lisa grew up on her family's cattle ranch in southern Arizona. Marriage and career took her to California and New Mexico, but the love of land and open space stayed with her. She returned to the ranch in 1993 and lived there until it was sold in 1998. She now divides her time between Tucson, Arizona and Taos, New Mexico.

See author's webpage: www.lisagsharp.com